A STORY OF HOPE

Lois Gray Miller &
Barbara Meekins Austin

A Story of Hope

Our Kinnakeet Heritage

Full-Service Book-Makers
Estd. 1999

PUBLISHED BY
The Chapel Hill Press, Inc., Chapel Hill, NC

ISBN 978-1-59715-253-2

First Printing
Printed in the United States of America

CONTENTS

FAITH OF OUR FATHERS

HISTORY

GENEALOGY

GOD'S MIRACULOUS WORKS

ANGELS

LIVELIHOOD

FRIENDS

MEMORIES OF A BYGONE ERA

AFTERNOON DELIGHTS

FAITH OF OUR FATHERS

LINEAGE FROM ABRAHAM TO JESUS

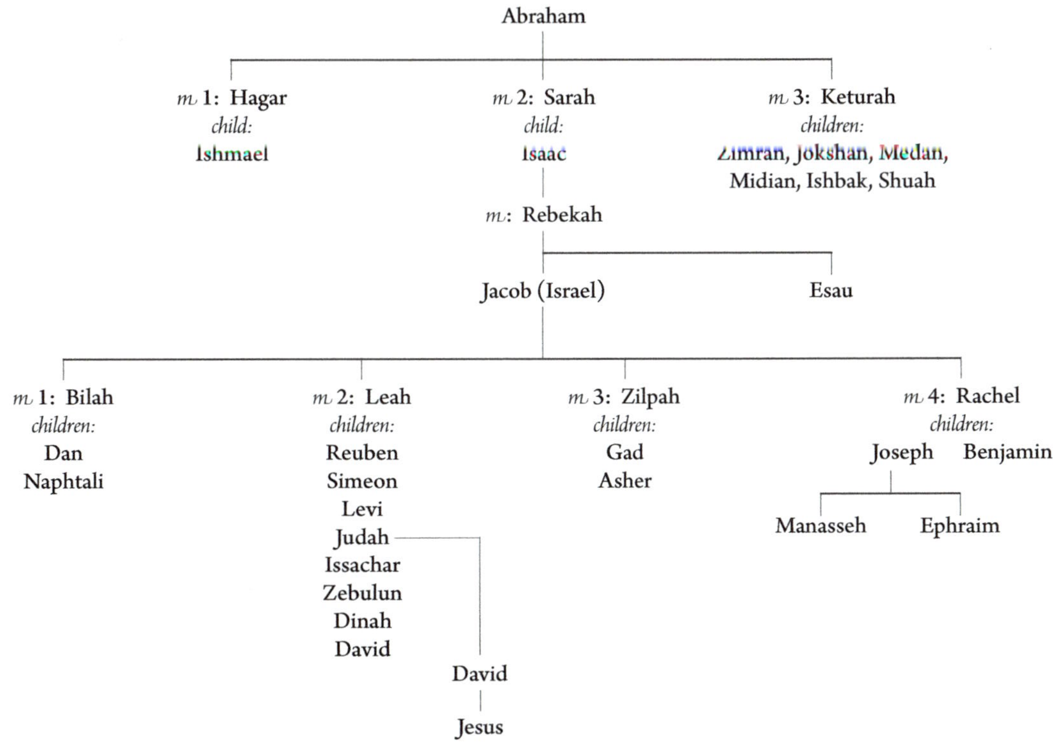

"IN THE BEGINNING"

In the Bible we see the book of Genesis as a book of literature, sacred text, and a science textbook. Genesis links the relationship between nations of the world and their ethnic origins. Genealogy confirms our historical roots and the unity we have. Genesis is highly regarded by the Jews, Christians, and Muslims who (through Ishmael, half-brother of Isaac) trace their spiritual heritage to Abraham.

When reading through the Bible, you will discover the greatest story ever told. "In the beginning" introduces God and the beginning of creation. In Genesis 11 we begin the cycle of Abraham with his call to migrate, his covenant with God, Sarah's barrenness, and the birth of Isaac. Genesis 18:12 tells us, "Sarah laughed." *Of course she did!* Sarah was a realist. God's promise was unbelievable from a human perspective. She reacted the way most of us would if we were in such a situation. There was no need for a pregnancy test, common sense told them that they were too old to have children (Abraham was 100 years old and Sarah was 90). But we can't hide any of our thoughts from the Lord. Isaac was born out of the laughter of disbelief. Isaac means, "He laughs." Have any of God's promises brought you to laughter?

The book of First Chronicles gives us a perspective on the history of God's people, showing how important it was for God's people to trace their roots and cling to their ancestral ties. There is a universal human need to belong. The Israelites were no different. Chronicles showed how the Israelites fit into God's plan. This genealogy connected the Israelites' return from exile with their ancestors and with the promises their ancestors had received from God.

Isaac's most famous descendant was Jesus. The first chapter of Matthew spends seventeen verses sharing genealogical names. Matthew puts the genealogy in to show that Jesus fulfilled the prophecy of the Old Testament. Jesus brought joy to many people during the time he walked the earth and has brought that joy to many more since he ascended. Sarah's laughter was not forced. It was a response to the news that she, a very old woman, would give birth to a son who would be part of Jesus' family tree.

Galatians 3:29 states, "Now that you belong to Christ, you are the true children of Abraham. You are his heirs, and God's promise to Abraham belongs to you." This is our heritage story of faith. First Peter 1:3–4 reads, "All praise to God, the Father of our Lord Jesus Christ. It is by His great mercy that we have been born again, because God raised Jesus Christ from the dead. Now we live with great expectation and we have a priceless inheritance—an inheritance that is kept in heaven for you, pure and undefiled, beyond the reach of change and decay."

Through the following stories we focus on how the promises to Abraham passed from generation to generation. This book illustrates the stories we tell today that will form our future but reflect our history. Our heritage is full of extraordinary stories about the ordinary people who opened their hearts to God and allowed the life, teachings, and person of Jesus Christ to transform them. We are guilty of not sharing the great stories of our spiritual ancestors. Let us rejoice and be glad that the traditions of our spiritual forefathers can freely be shared in this great land of freedom.

Christianity came to this country with the first colonist. In 1620 the Pilgrim fathers who risked their lives and limbs to cross the sea did so "for the glory of God and advancement of the Christian faith." Our early ancestors brought the principle of worship with them from their old countries.

The Baptists came in 1639; the Congregationalists, in 1648; the Lutherans and Episcopalians (Anglicans) began with the settlement of America; the Presbyterians came in 1703. The real founders of American Methodism were John Wesley and George Whitfield. Methodism was organized in America in 1743.

It is a historical fact that Methodism in all sections of our country was largely planted by southern men. What a heritage John Wesley, the founder of Methodism, has left us. He was born in 1703 and died in 1791. During the 65 years of his ministry it is estimated that he preached 42,000 times, published 200 books and pamphlets, and traveled 250,000 miles. Among his last words were, "The best of all is, God is with us," which he twice repeated.

CIRCUIT RIDERS IN COLONIAL TIMES

Circuit riders were Methodist preachers who traveled from place to place, community to community, carrying the Word of God. They preached the gospel, performed marriages, and baptized children. They traveled through all kinds of weather and had to contend with poor or uncertain lodging. They sometimes were blessed to be able to stay with sympathetic families, though at other times they had to sleep out in the open. Meetings were usually held in homes, schools, barns, or outdoors. Circuit riders usually went out on four-week circuits.

There were some very famous circuit riders, such as George Whitfield and even Bishop Francis Asbury himself. Many were less famous. My third great-grandfather Sylvaneous (Silvey) Meekins (1790–1873) was a circuit rider. He traveled around the area preaching. His son Dameron (Damon) G. Meekins was also a circuit rider. My aunt Brooksie Kuhl, in her book, *Stories of the Banks*, said that he traveled all over the Five Sounds area: Currituck, Albemarle, Roanoke, Pamlico, and Core Sound.

We read about the camp meetings held by circuit riders at Kings Point in Frisco and other parts of the island. I mention Kings Point because that is where Damon Meekins met his Indian wife, Laura Pamela Ward Stowe. People came from all over the island for these meetings. They came by boat, horse and cart, or on foot. They were hungry to hear the Word of God. They would make a camp and stay as long as the meetings lasted, sometimes two to three weeks.

When a community built a church and the district appointed a preacher, circuit riders were no longer needed.

I always heard that Silvey didn't receive a salary. Wondered if that was because no circuit rider received a salary or because he was not appointed. Maybe he felt the call of God on his life, picked up his Bible, got on his horse, and left to spread the gospel of Jesus Christ. When Silvey and his family appear in the 1850 census, he is listed as an M. E. (Methodist Episcopal) minister.

BARBARA MEEKINS AUSTIN

CHURCHES

Telling the Old, Old Story

Faith has always been at the center of life in Kinnakeet, as it was in every community on the Outer Banks. Settlers who resided in the village were without a house of worship. Before churches were built, people met in each other's homes to worship, and at that time children learned to read from the Bible. They continued to meet in homes and the school, which was near the outskirts of the village, when the circuit riders came through.

At a General Conference in 1844 the Methodist Church was split into the Methodist Episcopal Church South and Methodist Episcopal Church North. In Kinnakeet there were both. One was known simply as the Northern Methodist Church; the other was St. John Methodist Church. Not much is known about the Northern Methodist Church. According to Manson Meekins, the first church building was located on what is now C. C. Gray Circle, about where Clemmie Gray's house stands. The church was later moved, and a new building was built on North End Road. Mr. Meekins says their evening service was held at three in the afternoon. The young boys would hang out on the steps—especially when there were special meetings, because people, including young girls, would come from other villages. This church closed its doors in the early 1930s when the churches united. The building was bought by Ellis and Carrie Gray, converted into a home, and they lived there for many years.

Much history and many stories are told about St. John. One of my favorite stories is about how God provided so many oysters when it was decided that a church building was needed. In early September 1879, the villagers discovered an abundance of oysters in the area of Pamlico Sound known as Cape Channel. People came from Virginia and Maryland to buy the oysters. The people of Kinnakeet used every available boat to bring in the oysters to sell. In a short time there was enough money to buy lumber and other materials. The building was completed in 1880 and called South Banks Methodist (Episcopal). It later became St. John Methodist Episcopal Church South. The "South" was dropped from the name in 1939, and "Episcopal" was dropped in 1969. That building stood until 1960, when it was badly damaged by a hurricane. The present building was constructed in 1962.

In 1926 Pentecost came to the Outer Banks, brought by Myrtle Chambers and her husband, Charlie. Many people were drawn to this new form of worship. By 1931 a Pentecostal church was erected on a lot known as the Southard donated by Mr. and Mrs. Columbus Miller, not far from St. John Methodist Church. It was called Avon Pentecostal Church and had 44 members. Later it became affiliated with the Assembly of God and was named Avon Assembly of God Church. In the 1970s, while Rev. David Raynor was pastor, the name was changed to Avon Worship Center. Later still, it became the Faith Life Worship Center and currently is Heritage Church. In 1952–1953 the building was moved to its present location, on a lot across from Avon Harbor. The property was acquired from Rev. Alvin Price, a former pastor.

Miracles of salvation, healing, and other great works of God have been attributed to the churches of Avon, but for the church to recount what God has done in the past is not enough. We know that God is the Alpha and Omega, therefore we must also focus on the present and future. Let us savor the blessings and opportunities we have today and anticipate the thundering of the last trumpet sound when Christ will return.

BARBARA MEEKINS AUSTIN

St. John UMC 125th reunion artwork. Artwork by Cyril M. Gray Jr. (1937–2010)

The best mathematical equation I have ever seen: 1 cross + 3 nails = 4 given.

St. John United Methodist Church was first built in 1880. The new church was built in 1962.

The Pentecostal church in Avon was first located at the Southard. The church was moved to its current location on Harbor Road and is now known as Heritage Church. After the move, turnbuckles were attached by cables to the top corners of the church and were anchored in the sand for stabilization. The turnbuckles were from the shipwrecked schooner G. A. Kohler, *of 1933.*

I don't know why some people change churches; what difference does it make which one you stay home from?

Baptism of infant cousins: (L) Dorothy Miner holding Milah Scarborough Negrete; (R) Ruth Miner holding Lois Gray Miller

Dorothy C. and Ruth V. Miner, copastors of Avon Assembly of God Church, Avon, circa 1947

Some people are funny. They want the front of the bus, the middle of the road, and the back of the church.

HISTORY

BRIEF HISTORY OF KINNAKEET

The village of Avon, North Carolina, will be forever known in the hearts of Hatteras Islanders as Kinnakeet. As C. T. Williams II wrote in his wonderful book, *The Kinnakeeter,* the name comes from an Algonquian Indian term meaning "that which is mixed." Native American linguists at UNC-Pembroke have confirmed some basis for the definition.

Kinnakeet was the name of the Indian chief of present-day Avon at the time of John Lawson's arrival in July 1701. Lawson was the surveyor-general for the owners of the colony of Carolina, the Lords Proprietors. Lawson was astonished to find fair-skinned, blue-eyed, and freckled Indians among the natives. Lawson's reasoning for this was that survivors of the ill-fated Lost Colony in nearby Roanoke Island in 1587 relocated to Hatteras Island. Another plausible explanation for light-complected Indians is marooned shipwreck survivors heading for nearby Jamestown, Virginia, as early as 1607 who married into the Indian population. Lawson also recorded that he found an English Bible in their possession and that the Indians told him their ancestors could "talk in a book."

The earliest recorded landowner in Kinnakeet is Francis Farrow, who received a grant for almost the entire area of Avon in 1715. Farrow, an Irishman, had already been in the area for at least seven years. While local genealogists have traced Farrow's arrival to Maryland in the 1660s, it is speculated that he came here from the area of Goose Creek, near present-day Bath, North Carolina. Lawson and Farrow, a boatbuilder, likely knew each other, as Lawson laid out the area of Goose Creek for white settlement. Farrow and other early islanders moved here to escape the bloodbath in the Tuscarora Indian War of 1704–1715.

Farrow's 400-acre grant ran from Kinnacid Inlet, an old inlet near Ramp 34 north of Avon, to present-day Canadian Hole. Kinnakeet was full of magnificent cedars, which Kinnakeeters call juniper, perfect for boatbuilding. Farrow's great-grandson Pharoah Farrow Sr. became one of the wealthiest men in colonial Carolina, rafting these cedars out of the shallow inlet to waiting ships offshore, which carried it to New England and the thriving boatbuilding trade up there.

Kinnakeeters are among the finest small-boat watermen the world has ever produced, and they were in demand for their boatbuilding skills in colonial days on the mainland. In exchange for fresh produce, they bartered their skills and yaupon tea, which Kinnakeeters learned about from the Indians. Tea was hard to come by during the Revolution ,and preparing yaupon tea, a skill known exclusively among the earliest Kinnakeeters, was a task in high demand throughout colonial North Carolina.

It took an expert not only to make it correctly but also to cross Pamlico Sound and deliver a dry product to trade. The slightest moisture would render it unusable. Yaupon tea took some getting used to since it was an inferior substitute for the real thing. It smelled good while brewing and served to overpower unpleasant odors milling around the homestead from various livestock in the yard, which ran free and unfenced until the 1930s.

Kinnakeet made great contributions to our country's freedom in the Revolutionary War, the War of 1812, the Civil War, World Wars I and II, and in Korea and Vietnam. It is a well-known fact that Kinnakeet has contributed military personnel to every war our great county has ever fought in defense of freedom. Kinnakeeters are especially proud of the fact that they were the earliest southerners to reject the Confederacy in favor of the Union. Patriotic Kinnakeeters saw no need to dissolve our country just 75 years after their grandfathers had fought to free us from England.

Dare County was formed on February 3, 1870, from Currituck, Tyrrell, and Hyde Counties. Currituck County was created in 1668 from Albemarle County (originally named Carteret Precinct, declared Carteret County in 1739). Although Dare was formed in 1870, its history goes back to 1585, when England made its first attempt to settle in the New World.

The county is named after Virginia Dare, the first child born of English parents in America. Dare is in the eastern section of the state, bounded by Pamlico, Croatan, and Albemarle Sounds, Hyde and Tyrrell Counties, and the Atlantic Ocean.

Manson Meekins' interview with the National Park Service gives a description of old Avon. Today's Harbor Road did not exist before World War II, and the harbor area was a swamp. "The creek in the middle of the swamp ran from Pamlico Sound right up through the village, separating Dog Ridge [southern half] from Cat Ridge [northern side]." Kinnakeeters referred to "Cat Ridgers" and "Dog Ridgers," and joked that the names came about because families living in those areas "fought like cats and dogs." A cart path and footbridge connected Cat Ridge and Dog Ridge before the mouth of the creek was dug out in 1947 to form the harbor and the surrounding marshy area was filled. The east edge of the village bordering the swamp was called the Hills. An area farther south was called Pot Head, and a collection of houses on the northern border was referred to as the North'ard or Spain. A mile south of the village beyond Pot Head was once a settlement called the South'ard.

According to a report by the Cape Hatteras National Park Service, in the 1700s Kinnakeet was home to the Scarborough, Price, Williams, Miller, Farrow, Meekins, and Hooper families: later the Gray name also became prominent. For most of its early existence, Kinnakeet was the largest village on all of Hatteras Island. In 1846, a violent storm created Hatteras Inlet and made Hatteras Village the economic center of Hatteras Island.

GENEALOGY

FROM DNA TO GENEALOGY

Genealogy is derived from two Greek words that combined mean "family science" or "the study of family." It is a process used to gather information about ancestral relations to establish a historical family tree. In the past, as well as today, this information is primarily established through the written record (birth certificates, chart pedigrees, records in books or Bibles), along with visits to libraries, courthouses, and graveyards, and oral communication with relatives and friends.

In recent years, due to technological advancements, we have the ability to chemically analyze our genetic hereditary materials. In doing so, DNA testing—which looks at specific regions on the structures (chromosomes) that carry our DNA—can be used to aid in establishing ancestral relationships. To a lesser degree of accuracy, the ethnic mixture of an individual can be estimated. This statistical, analytical process of study has resulted in the development of a new discipline called genetic genealogy. To understand the concepts of this process, one must have a general knowledge of DNA and how it works. That is the purpose of this chapter, so let's begin!

DNA is an acronym for an organic (carbon-based) molecule called deoxyribonucleic acid. It functions as the genetic material of all life on earth. Regardless of whether an organism is a bacterium, a plant, an animal, a human, or something else. DNA is what forms the genes controlling hereditary traits. We focus here on its application to human genetics and genealogy.

How does DNA work? In simplistic terms, DNA contains the hereditary code passed from generation to generation via the sperm and egg. It permits the offspring (baby) to synthesize proteins.

Why is it important? Let's briefly discuss background information needed to answer this question.

Proteins play diverse roles in a body's anatomy (structure) and physiology (chemical function). Structurally, proteins help in forming cell membranes, and fiber in muscle cells that permit muscle organs to contract; hair and nail formation; bone stability; formation of tendons and ligaments; and much more. Chemically, proteins compose antibodies for protection from disease and enzymes for regulating the rate of chemical reactions such as digestion, synthesis of some hormones, and much more.

Let's elaborate on the synthesis and functions of the protein enzymes. First, the DNA of the sperm and egg unite. The resulting fertilized egg (biologist call this a zygote) then begins a process controlled by the DNA called protein synthesis. As the term implies, the DNA genetic code initiates the production of a large variety of protein molecules, including the enzymes. Enzymes regulate the physiological processes associated with growth and development of the offspring. They control the rate of chemical reactions, permitting them to occur fast enough to support all life processes. Without enzymes, life processes would almost spontaneously come to a grinding halt.

In summary, we inherit from our parents DNA in the form of chromosomes (discussed shortly). The DNA then regulates production of proteins. Proteins then regulate the body's structural and functional development. Without DNA, no proteins; without protein, no life!

What do we mean when we say "chromosome" or "gene" in relation to DNA? Molecules of DNA are composed of smaller molecules that link together in linear strands. These smaller building-block molecules are called nucleotides. Therefore, a DNA molecule is simply a chain of nucleotides, much like a pearl necklace is a chain of pearls linked together by a string or cord. Let's say a DNA molecule is formed from 50 million nucleotides linked together with the aid of some protein molecules. The resulting DNA/protein structure is a chromosome. The largest human chromosome is composed of about 250 million nucleotides!

Although it takes millions of nucleotides to compose one chromosome, there are actually only four different types of DNA nucleotides. Different sequences of these four nucleotides on a chromosome regulate the synthesis of a specific type of protein. Each sequence that regulates the synthesis of a protein is called a gene. Therefore, a gene for eye color is a nucleotide sequence on part of a chromosome that regulates production of protein molecules that, for example, result in a person having brown eyes instead of blue.

Another example would be as follows: We need a protein enzyme called lactase that permits us to digest a sugar in dairy products called lactose. Humans have a sequence of nucleotides (a gene) on one of the chromosomes that regulates synthesis of lactose. Thus, we can consume the sugar lactose, digest it, and use it for energy. Some people inherit a defective form of this gene and cannot produce lactase, so they cannot properly digest lactose and may experience undesired and uncomfortable side effects when consuming dairy products—lactose intolerance.

A small chromosome may contain a few hundred genes. The largest human chromosome contains over 2,000 genes. It is estimated that the human genome (an organism's complete set of DNA and its genes) contain 20,000 to 25,000 genes located on 23 pairs of chromosomes. These genes regulate all protein synthesis and therefore all life processes!

In a normal human cell (other than sperm or egg) there are 23 types of chromosomes that occur in pairs. Thus, a total of 46 chromosomes regulate life processes. When a sperm cell or an egg cell is formed, only one of each chromosomal type is placed into the sex cell (biologists call sperm and egg cells gametes.). The result is that the sperm that fertilizes an egg will pass on to its offspring one of each type of the father's chromosomes. This is true for the egg as well. The resulting fertilized egg will get half (23) of its chromosomes from the father and the other half from the mother. This process reestablishes the complete complement of 23 pairs of chromosomes with the genes needed to regulate growth, development, and maintenance of the offspring.

The 23 pairs of chromosomes discussed so far are located in a part of each human cell called the nucleus. We can refer to this as nuclear DNA. Cells also have structures called mitochondria that regulate how we can convert food to energy. Each mitochondrion contains up to 10 circular chromosomes with their specific genes needed to accomplish this task. We can call this mitochondrial DNA. Sperm cells do not contribute mitochondria when fertilizing an egg: the egg cell already has its own mitochondria. As such, male and female offspring contain mitochondrial DNA inherited from only their mother. In genetic genealogy, mitochondrial DNA can be used to test matrilineal (mother's) ancestry as far back as 52 generations. In comparison, nuclear DNA can be used to trace ancestry with reasonable results for about five to six generations, unless it is the nuclear DNA of chromosome number 23. This chromosome is called the Y-chromosome and contains a male-determining gene that can be used to test patrilineal (father's) ancestry back about 25 generations.

What do we mean when we say "Y-chromosome"? Of the 23 pairs of nuclear chromosomes, only one pair determines gender of the offspring. This pair is referred to as the sex chromosomes. One type of sex chromosome is called the Y-chromosome. It has a gene that initiates the development of male reproductive structures. The other type of sex chromosome is called an X-chromosome. It regulates the development of female reproductive structures.

A normal male sex chromosome composition is one Y-chromosome plus one X-chromosome (XY). The Y-chromosome has one sex-determining gene that can override several genes on the X-chromosome resulting in the development of male structures.

A normal female sex chromosome composition is two X-chromosomes (XX). Due to lack of a Y-chromosome, the X-chromosome genes produce a female.

As previously mentioned, this means the Y-chromosome, found in males only, can be used in genealogy to trace patrilineal ancestry.

In summary, we have attempted to explain what DNA is and how it works, how genes that regulate body structure and function are passed from one generation to the next, and how this knowledge can be used to aid genealogy studies. This process is still not 100 percent understood, but enough is understood to have meaningful applications to heredity and supplement the establishment of a family tree.

Numerous companies offer in-home kits that permit one to submit, for example, a cheek swab sample that can be used to derive and analyze one's DNA. The accuracy of these tests is variable and debatable. I recommend researching the reputation of these companies and comparing costs before choosing.

It may be interesting to note that we are all 99.5 percent to 99.9 percent genetically the same. The remaining 0.1 percent to 0.5 percent make us individually unique!

COLLINS GRAY JR., PROFESSOR OF BIOLOGY

FARROW

Francis Farrow 1667–1721
*(*First Farrow in Eastern NC) Largest island grant holder*
Birth–Middlesex (London), England
1683 Arrived in Maryland
Death–Currituck NC (current Dare County, Avon, NC)
m. Barbary Guthrie 1670–

Children of Francis Farrow

Daniel Guthrie
1700–1752
m. Bethany J. Bannister

Hezekiah
1747–1811
m. Elizabeth

Captain Jacob 1705–1785
Served in the House of Commons 1760–62
m. Amy Swindel 1710–1782
some research states Jacob had 2 wives, one named Amy and one named Elizabeth
Elizabeth was the wife of Hezekiah's son Jacob II

Isaac
1707–
m. Catherine

Children of Hezekiah

Thomas
1717–

Hezekiah D.
1805–1858
m. Christiana

Samuel I
1794–

Pelege Spencer
1809–

Angelica Barnett
1790–

Mourning
1810–

Silas
1790–

Edward
1801–1839
m. Mary
1771–1834
child:
Hezekiah David
1831–1887

Jacob Jr. (II)
1801–*c.* 1850
m. Elizabeth 1806–
children:
Thomas,
Hezekiah John,
Elizabeth,
Barbara

Loranzo Burrus
1811–1869
Eliza
1817–

Francis Farrow 1667–1721
m Barbary Guthrie 1670–

- Daniel Guthrie 1700–1752 *m* Bethany J. Bannister
- Hezekiah 1747–1811 *m* Elizabeth
- Captain Jacob 1705–1785 *m* Amy Swindel 1710–1782
  - *children of Captain Jacob and Amy Farrow*
  - Isaac I 1732–
  - Mary Brooks 1730–1795 *m* Stephen Brooks 1728–1795
  - Rosiman Perkins 1736–
  - Pheby Morse 1738–
  - Sarah Hancock 1740–
  - Barbary (Barbara) Phillips 1742–
  - Comfort 1740–1783 *m* Joseph Williams 1705–1775 *children:* Caleb, Joseph, Jacob, James and Robert
  - Francis Farrow II *c.* 1740–1815 *m* Esther I
    Daughter: Ester II married Joseph Morgan, daughter Mourning Morgan (1805–*c.* 1840) *m* Jesse O'Neal 1803–1870
  - Thomas 1756–1789
- Isaac 1707– *m* Catherine
  - Isaac Jr. 1746– *m* Unknown
  - Jacob
  - Christopher 1765–1806 *m* Nancy
    children: David, Barshaba, Mahala, Delora, Lydia, Nancy
  - Joseph
  - Abraham

*Pharoah Farrow 1770–1840
m1. Rasmine (native American) 1806–1816
m2. Elizabeth
m3. Rosanah Elizabeth Swindell Scarborough 1770–1861
m4. Mary Polly
m5. Sarah
children of Pharoah:

John Pharoah 1813–*c.* 1846	*m.* Sarah Murphy	*children:* John Alfred I 1874–1957, Cyrus H., Clifford L., Melissa Ann 1872–1958, Celia A., Louvenia
Abraham 1793–1847	*m.* Sara Sally Meekins	*children:* Isaac K. *m.* Elizabeth Credle, Sally *m.* H.F. Barnett Jr., Esther *s:* Ignatious Scarborough, Rosemon 1812–1845 possibly another son named Abram
Isaac L. 1803–1842	*m.* Dorcas Gray	*children:* Brittany 1828– *m.* Bateman Price, Mary R. 1833–1916 *m.* Cyrus Hooper
—*twins*—		
Christopher Cross 1803–1850	*m.* Jane Williams	*children:* Abraham 1824–1870, Louisa T. 1826–, Rosetta 1830–, Rosannah 1832–, Olivia 1834–, Redding 1836–1864
Christian 1797–1846	*m.* William Scarborough 1764–1824	*children:* William Jr., Banister 1817–1890, John 1826–, Stancil 1812–1874, Pharoah 1829–, Elizabeth Jane (Betsy) 1836–1870 *m.* Anderson Gray
Eliza 1805		
Clifford 1800–1838	*m.* Sarah	
Polly A. 1818–1850	*m.* Hezekiah Barnett 1813–1866	*child:* David 1851–
Elizabeth 1821–1889	*m1.* 2nd spouse of Davis Gray 1829–1901	
	m2. Little Abner Gray 1837–1880	*children with Abner:* Elizabeth Abner, Lavinia, Olive Francis
Caroline B. 1824		
Rosemon 1820–1880	*m.* Stancil Scarborough 1812–1874	*children:* Farrow Langford 1854–1926, Mary Christian 1850–1929, Brittania 1844–1876, William 1847–1871, Sarah 1850–, Amy 1857 *died young*
Napolian Howard 1828–1847	*m.* Anna W. Midgette *c.* 1826–1857 *(Anna's 2nd husband–Henderson Scarborough)*	
Dorcas G. 1820–1849		
Jane 1829–1850	*m1.* William Allen Gray	
	m2. Jesse Gray 1824–1892	*child with Jesse:* Zachariah 1848–1889

**Some genealogists speculate that Pharoah was the son of the eldest Abraham or possibly the son of Isaac Sr. Due to deterioration of wooden grave markers research is inconclusive but according to Hubert Price, a bible in possesion of a Farrow family member states Pharoah Farrow was the son of Isaac Jr. Soooo Pharoah Farrow, who's your daddy?*

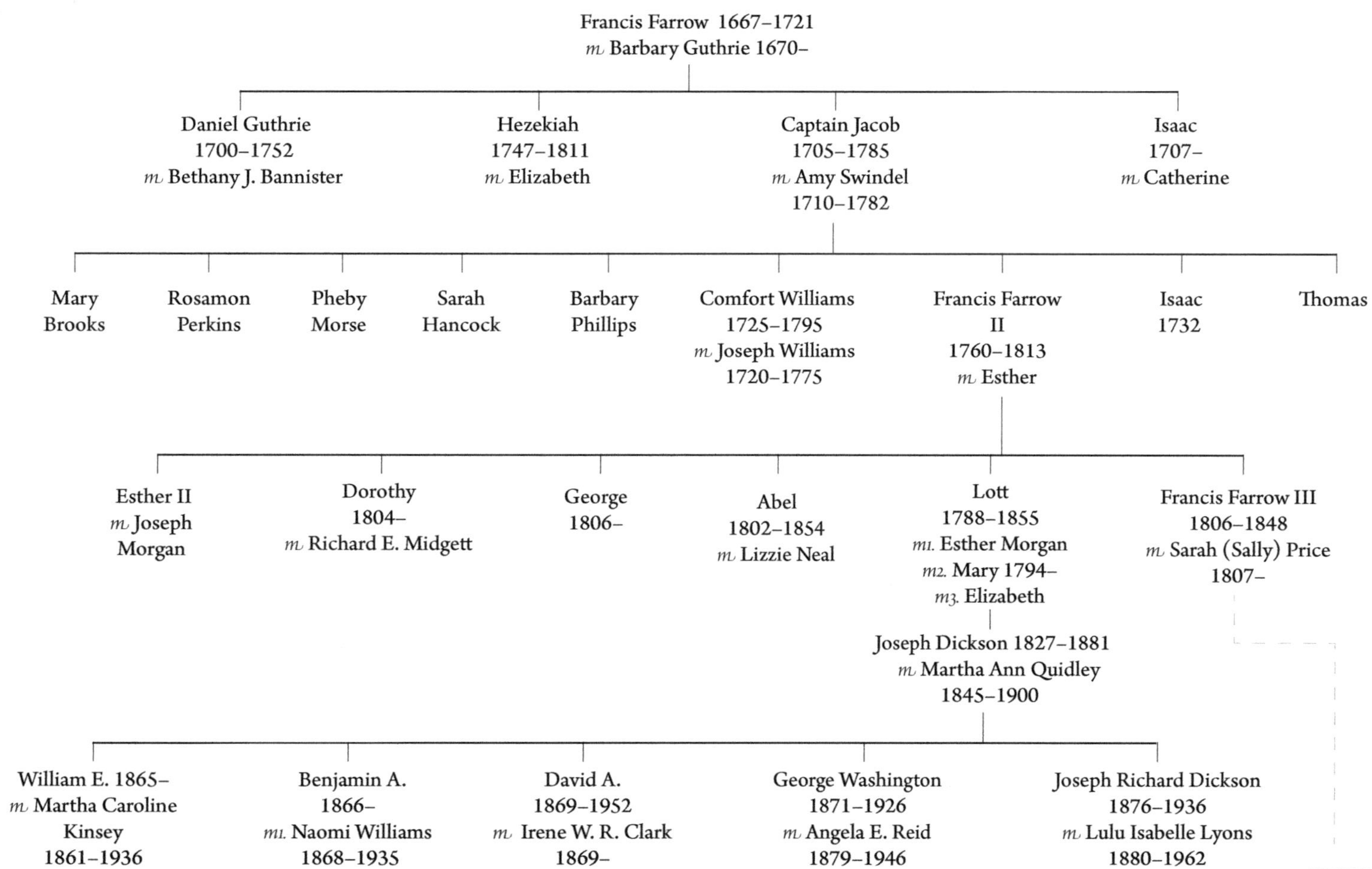

Francis Farrow 1667–1721
m. Barbary Guthrie 1670–
Daniel Guthrie
1700–1752
m. Bethany J. Bannister
Hezekiah
1747–1811
m. Elizabeth
Captain Jacob
1705–1785
m. Amy Swindel
1710–1782
Isaac
1707–
m. Catherine
Mary
Brooks
Rosamon
Perkins
Pheby
Morse
Sarah
Hancock
Barbary
Phillips
Comfort Williams
1725–1795
m. Joseph Williams
1720–1775
Francis Farrow
II
1760–1813
m. Esther
Isaac
1732
Thomas
Esther II
m. Joseph
Morgan
Dorothy
1804–
m. Richard E. Midgett
George
1806–
Abel
1802–1854
m. Lizzie Neal
Lott
1788–1855
m1. Esther Morgan
m2. Mary 1794–
m3. Elizabeth
Francis Farrow III
1806–1848
m. Sarah (Sally) Price
1807–
Joseph Dickson 1827–1881
m. Martha Ann Quidley
1845–1900
William E. 1865–
m. Martha Caroline
Kinsey
1861–1936
Benjamin A.
1866–
m1. Naomi Williams
1868–1935
David A.
1869–1952
m. Irene W. R. Clark
1869–
George Washington
1871–1926
m. Angela E. Reid
1879–1946
Joseph Richard Dickson
1876–1936
m. Lulu Isabelle Lyons
1880–1962

children of Francis III and Sarah Price Farrow:

Emaline Christian
1829–1866
1st wife of
Selby M. Gray
1832–1882

Richard Gray Farrow
1831–1912
m. Celia Ann Gray
1839–1903

1. Emaline 1864–1890
   m. Levin B. Gray 1865–1935
   children: Maria "Nina", Callista (Lessie)
2. Major Everett 1882–1959
   m. Melvinia Williams 1884–1963
3. Rutherford Hayes 1877–1943
   m. Mary Belle Foster 1884–1908
4. Fannie Miller 1860–1925
   m. William Bembry Miller 1850–1921
5. Celia R. 1866–
6. Margaret Ann 1869–
   m. Stephen B. Gray 1868–1920
   children: Emaline, Rutherford B., Louise E., Cecilia, Mary (Mamie)
7. Rosemane 1869–

Francis Farrow IV
1832–1912
m. Mary E. Casey
1842–

1. Hulda Ann 1871–1951
   m. Wesley Collins Willians 1872–1920 *children:* Edward, Percy, Claude, Selina, Annie
2. Mary Jane Gray 1867–
   m. Frank Gray
3. Lancaster 1869–
4. William (*died young*)

George
died young

Selina Barnes
1834–
died young

Lancaster Midgett Farrow
1836–1881
m. Dorcas Hooper
1813

1. John Devine 1875–1934
   m. Willie Ann Gray 1878–1954
   children: Emma, Dorcas, Lucy
2. Wilson (Wilse) 1878–1951
   never married
3. Lorenzo "Ranzey" Dowe 1873–1929
   m. Julia D. Midgett 1875–1931
   children: Perry, John, David

GRAY

The Gray family in the United States is numerous, widespread and consists of many diverse branches. They were among the Pilgrims of New England, the Quakers of Pennsylvania and the early settlers of VA and other southern states. Within the first century, between 1620 and 1720, research indicates that there were at least twenty different families of Grays, or different branches of the same family, which had emigrated to this country and made their homes in the New World.

William Gray
land grant at Little Kinnakeet c. early 1700s

- Thomas Gray 1750–1790 *m.* Charity Buskirk 1755–
- William II *c.* 1755–

Children of Thomas Gray and Charity Buskirk:

- Stephen Gray 1791–1860 *m.* Nancy Gray 1790–1850
- Abner H. Gray 1775–1850 *m.* Marguerite Mars 1782–1870 *(Abner and Marguerite married at St. Gabriel, Louisiana)*

Children of Abner H. Gray and Marguerite Mars:

- Mahala 1801–1870
- Davis Littleton 1806–1881 *m.* Laurana Midyett 1815–1847
- Mary Louise 1809–1850 *m.* Ira B. Midgett 1806–1870
- Joshua Gray 1808–1891 *m.* Sabrina Brady 1810–1885
- Anderson 1814–1858 *m.* Mary P. Scarborough 1813–1860
- Nathan 1825–1880 *m.* Mary W. Meekins 1821–
- *Bethany 1811–1891 *m.* Ezekiel Hooper 1801–1855

**see Hooper pedigree chart*

Son of Davis Littleton:

Bannister Midgett Gray (Red Ban) 1833–1912

m1. Mary Midgett
chldren:
Henrietta M. 1860 *died young*
Elizabeth M. 1862–1867
William (Bill) Hawkins 1865– *m.* Melissa Farrow

m2. Rosa Meekins 1847–1933 *(daughter of Isaac and Nancy Meekins)*
children:
Ignatious M. 1869–1924 *m.* Margaret Etheridge Scarborough
Bateman M. 1870–
Mary 1872–
Louisa Christian 1875–1910
Esther 1877–
Caroline Wilson 1878–1953 *m.* William Bembry Miller
Rebecca 1880–
Margaret 1884–1912

William Gray
land grant at Little Kinnakeet c. early 1700s

- **Thomas Gray 1750–1790**
  m. Charity Buskirk 1755–
  - **Stephen Gray 1791–1860**
    m. Nancy Gray 1790–1850
  - **Abner H. Gray 1775–1850**
    m. Marguerite Mars 1782–1870
    (Abner and Marguerite married at St. Gabriel, Louisiana)
    - **Mahala**
      1801–1870
    - **Davis Littleton**
      1806–1881
      m. Laurana Midyett
      1815–1847
    - **Mary Louise**
      1809–1850
      m. Ira B. Midgett
      1806–1870
    - **Joshua Gray**
      1808–1891
      m. Sabrina Brady
      1810–1885
      - **Bethany S.**
        1830–1891
        Deaf Mute
      - **Anderson "Little"**
        1832–1905
        m1. Elizabeth Jane Scarborough
        m2. Elizabeth S. Hooper
        children with Elizabeth Scarborough:
        Malachi Littleton
        Mathew Jordan
        child with Elizabeth Hooper:
        Joshua Gibbs
      - **Malachi**
        1834–1881
        m1. Adeline Pugh
        m2. Elizabeth Gray
        children with Adeline:
        Tilman Pugh
        Franklin T.
        Anderson
        children with Elizabeth:
        Elizabeth
        Sabra Ann
      - **Allen W.**
        1838–1907
        Kittura Midgett "Kitty"
        1833–1876
        children:
        Nathan P.
        Shanklin W.
        Christopher
        Levin B.
      - **Sanders P.**
        1840–1906
        m1. Charlotte Gray
        1842–1886
        m2. Catherine Rebecca Hooper Meekins
        1846–1915
        children with Charlotte:
        Ema
        Joseph Mitchell
      - **Banister B.**
        1842–1916
        m1. Brittania Scarborough
        1844–1876
        m2. Sarah Gray
        1850–1915
        children with Brittania:
        William W.
        children with Sarah:
        Anne, David
      - **Levin B.**
        1848–1913
        Louisa Gray
        1856–1900
        children:
        Benjamin
        William Brinkley
        Allen B.
      - **Ezekiel C.**
        1848–1880
      - **Anna H.**
        1850–1896
        2nd wife of Ervin H. Williams
        1850–1919
    - **Anderson**
      1814–1858
      m. Mary P. Scarborough
      1813–1860
    - **Nathan**
      1825–1880
      m. Mary W. Meekins
      1821–
    - ***Bethany 1811–1891**
      m. Ezekiel Hooper
      1801–1855
      **see Hooper pedigree chart*
- **William II** *c.* 1755–

Thomas Gray 1750–1790
m. Charity Buskirk 1755–

- Stephen Gray 1791–1860
  m. Nancy Gray 1790–1850
- Abner H. Gray 1775–1850
  m. Marguerite Mars 1782–1870
  (Born Lafourche, Louisiana)
  - Mahala
    1801–1870
  - Nathan N.
    1825–1880
  - Mary Louise
    1809–1850
  - Joshua Gray
    1808–1891
  - Anderson
    1814–1858
    m. Mary P. Scarborough
    1813–1860
    - Robert Watson
      1837–1913
      m. Hulda Ann Price
      1844–1913
      children:
      Polly Ann 1866
      George Max 1869
      Bethany B. 1871
      Oliver (Obbie) J. 1873
      Bateman W. 1875 *died young*
      Hosania S. *died young*
      David Watson *died young*
    - Sabra Ann Gray
      1840–1860
      1st wife of:
      Isaac James Williams
      1834–1917
      child:
      Sabra Ann W. Miller
    - Oliver N.
      1842–1901
      Rhoda Scarborough
      1849–1869
      m2. Elizabeth Gibbs
      1840–1899
      m3. Zurlina Williams
      children:
      Nancy Jane G. Williams
      Mary Wallace G. O'Neal
      Elizabeth Gibbs
    - Comfort
      1844–1868
      m. James Ignatious
      Quidley
      1844–1913
    - Anderson Littleton
      1852–1908
      m1. Mary "Mavey" C. Meekins
      1855–1887
      m2. Cordelia Price
      1866–1955
      children with Mary Christian:
      Rody Ann 1880–1889
      Dameron Nelson 1880–1960
      Comfort V. Price 1877–1939
      children with Cordelia:
      Willis Brown 1891–1955
      Missouri G. Meekins 1894–1983
      Beulah G. Scarborough 1897–1974
      Nicodemas 1899–1968
      Edward Watson 1906–1986
  - Davis Littleton
    1806–1881
  - Bethany
    1811–1891

Thomas Gray 1750–1790
m. Charity Buskirk 1755–

Stephen Gray 1791–1860
m. Nancy Gray 1790–1850

Abner H. Gray 1775–1850
m. Marguerite Mars 1782–1870
(Born Lafourche, Louisiana)

Mahala
1801–1870

Mary Louise
1809–1850
m. Ira B. Midgett
1806–1870

Joshua Gray
1808–1891

Anderson
1814–1858

Davis Littleton
1806–1881

Bethany
1811–1891

Nathan N.
1825–1880

"Little" Nichodemus
1828–1901
m. Effica S. Meekins
1830–1912
children:
Mary Little
Little Nichodemus
Dameron
John Pugh
James Meekins
William Washington
Jeremiah
Jack M.
Anna Eliza

Dameron G.
1834–1900
m. Cordelia
1836–1912

Arcade A.
1830–*after* 1850

Ebenezer
1839–1905
m. Mary Spencer
Hooper
1847–1919
child:
Sarah H.

Ira Brock Jr.
1839–1870
m. Margaret R.
1837–1906
children:
Henry Vernon
Abraham Franklin
Mary Louisa

George Washington
1846–1871
m. Nancy Thomas O'Neal
1843–
child:
George Brinton
McClellan

Nathan O.
1845–1873
m. Ann Wetherington
1852–1929
**Ann later married*
Davis L. Gray

Thomas Gray 1750–1790
m. Charity Buskirk 1755–

Stephen Gray 1791–1860
m. Nancy Gray 1790–1850

Abner H. Gray 1775–1850
m. Marguerite Mars 1782–1870

Thomas Gray
1815–1906
m. Dorcas L. Barnes
1816–1882

Davis Gray
1829–1901
m1. Deliah Scarborough
–1881
m2. 1st husband of
Elizabeth H. Farrow Gray
1821–1889
m3. Polly A. Basnight
–1888
m4. Martha Ann Williams
1855–1929

Abner H. Gray
1837–1880
m. 2nd husband of
Elizabeth H. Far-
row Gray
1821–1889
children:
Elizabeth Abner
Lavinia
Olive Frances

Elizabeth
1832–

John B.
1842–*c.* 1880
Sabra Miller
1848–1914
children:
Joseph 1873
Noah 1875
David 1877

Jesse N.
1824–1892
m1. Jane Farrow
m2. Elsie Styron

Mary H.
1841–1866
m. 1st. wife of
Bateman Miller
1841–1911
child:
Jones L. Miller
1864–1948

Jesse Gray
1845–1922
m. Rosetta (Rosa) Mann
Scarborough Gray
1846–1939

Elizabeth
1831–1917

Lorenzo (Rans) Hooper Gray 1869–1944
m1. Lizzie Price Gray 1905–
m2. Amelia Ann Quidley Gray 1872–1941

John Allen Gray 1875–1965
m. Brittania Williams Gray 1882–1958

Thomas Gray 1750–1790
m. Charity Buskirk 1755–

Stephen Gray 1791–1860
m. Nancy Gray 1790–1850

Abner H. Gray 1775–1850
m. Marguerite Mars 1782–1870

Thomas Gray
1815–1906

Davis Gray
1829–1902

Abner H. Gray
1837–1880

Elizabeth
1832–

John B.
1842–*c.* 1880

Jesse N.
1824–1892
m1. Jane Farrow
1829–1850
m2. Elsie Styron
1831–

son of Jane:
Zachariah P.
1848–1889
m. Sarah R. Scarborough
1855–1939
children:
William J.
Elveretta R.
Elmetta
Jesse Thomas

daughter of Elsie:
Jane Gray
1852–1920
m. William Allen Gray
1849–1913
children:
Dorther James Gray
Charlie

son of Elsie:
Farrow S.
1854–1890
m. Nancy Barnes
1857–1923

daughter of Elsie:
Louisa Ballance
1856–1900
m. Levin B. Gray
1848–1913
children:
Benjamin 1876–1956
William Brinkley 1877–1968
Allen 1885–1908

son of Elsie:
Stephen B.
1868–1920
m. Margaret A. Farrow
1869–
children:
Sarah L. 1888–1905
Emaline 1891–1926
Rutherford B. 1896–1967
Louisa E. 1902–1917
Cecilia 1908–1990
Mary (Mamie) 1889–1993

Sarah 1878–1918
never married

Louis B. 1880–1917
never married

Menville Lucretia 1882–1959
m. David Fields Meekins 1883–1963

Bannister B. 1895–1919
m. Blanch Rulan 1892–1984

Thomas Gray 1750–1790 *m.* Charity Buskirk 1755–

Abner Gray 1775–1850 *m.* Marguerite Mars 1785–1870

Anderson Gray 1814–1858 *m.* Mary Polly Scarborough 1813–1860

Robert Watson Gray 1837–1913 *m.* Hulda Ann Price 1844–1913

Hosania	David Watson	Polly Ann	George Maxwell	Bethaney B.	Oliver James	Bateman
1862–1863	1865–1866	1866–1885	1869–1918	1871–1888	1873–1940	1875–1885
died young	*died young*	*m.* Thomas Gray 1856–1921	*m.* Montra C. Meekins 1870–1949	*1st. wife of:* Cyrus Richard Hooper 1865–1941	*m.* Mary W. Midgett 1876–1954	*died young*

Children of George Maxwell:

Columbus Castevens	Willie Bateman	Thomas James	Annie Brown	Lewis M	Joseph Curtis	Lucy M.	Carrie Winston
1891–1966	1892–1973	1894–1961	1896–1984	1899–1954	1901–1962	1903–1984	1905–2007
m. Esta Taylor Meekins 1893–1982	*m.* Ersie Gray 1890–1979	*m.* Achsah M. Williams 1897–1994	*m1.* Elmore Gray 1896–1924 *m2.* Warren Robinson Midgett	*m1.* Gracie Farrow 1901–1920 *m2.* Mae Gray	*m.* Minnie Miller 1903–1997	*m.* Mack T. Gray 1896–1984	*m.* Talmage O'Neal 1900–1939

Thomas Gray 1750–1790 *m.* Charity Buskirk 1755–

Abner Gray 1775–1850 *m.* Marguerite Mars 1785–1870

Anderson Gray 1814–1858 *m.* Mary Polly Scarborough 1813–1860

Robert Watson Gray 1837–1913 *m.* Hulda Ann Price 1844–1913

Hosanna S.	David Watson	Polly Ann	George Maxwell	Bethaney B.	Oliver James	Bateman
1862–1863	1865–1866	1866–1885	1869–1918	1871–1888	1873–1940	1875–1885
died young	*died young*	*m.* Thomas Gray 1856–1921	*m.* Montra C. Meekins 1870–1949	*3rd wife of:* Cyrus Richard Hooper 1865–1941	*m.* Mary W. Midgett 1876–1954	*died young*

children of Oliver (Obbie) and Mary Gray:
Lovie Ann Gray Gray 1897–1944 *2nd. wife of:* Eugene Grandberry Gray 1889–1966
Willard James 1894–1969 *1st. Spouse:* Eunice May Hooper 1893–1967 *2nd. Spouse:* Beatrice Hogan *c.* 1895–1988
Robert Watson 1908–1989 *m.* Isabella Williams Scarborough 1911–1959 Lillian P. Gray Miller 1899–1984 *m.* Bateman P. Miller 1876–
Ellis Andrew 1902–1989 *m.* Caroline Mythilda Rowland 1914–2005
Oliver James Gray Jr. 1904–1978 *m.* Christine Williams 1906–1982
Amelia Gray 1907–1908 *died young*
Amanda Gray Gray 1907–1985 *m.* Burgess Anderson Gray 1902–1988
Edward S. 1910–1911 *died young*
Cyril Midgett 1914–1980 *m.* Grace Gray 1914–1992
John "Jack" Berchman Gray 1927–1997 *m.* Anna Scarborough 1934–2011
(John son of Willard J. and Beatrice Hogan Gray, raised by Oliver and Mary Gray)

William Gray
[land grant at Little Kinnakeet c. early 1700s]

Thomas Gray
1750–1790
m Charity Buskirk
1755–

William II
c. 1755–
m Unknown

Richard *c.* 1772
m Unknown

Dorcas
m Isaac L. Farrow
1802–1842

Ezekiel Gray
c. 1794–*c.* 1848
Christian Jane Williams
1796–*c.* 1881

Sarah
m Francis Farrow III
1806–1848

Wallace Gray 1822–1899
m Cynthia Price 1828–1917
(daughter of Noah Price Sr.)

Tilmon J. Gray 1857–1897
m Lucinda J. Farrow 1855–1950
(daughter of Ervin and Willie Miller Farrow)

Willie Ann Gray 1878–1954
m John Devine Farrow 1875–1934
(son of Lancaster Midgett Farrow)
children:
Emma Gray, Dorcas Meekins, Lucy Miller

HOOPER

Ezekiel Hooper 1712–
[*Bodie Island, Currituck, NC, US*]
m. Catherine Midyett 1716–*c.* 1776

Rowan 1734–1790
[*Chicamacomico*]

Ezekiel 1756–1827
[*Kinnakeet, NC*]
m. Comfort Williams

- Cyrus
  1795–1885
  m1. Mary Ann Gray
  m2 Dorcas Payne
  m3. Sarah Caffee
  children:
  Andrew Shanklin 1840–1917
  Edward 1845–
  Jeremiah 1859–1933
  Richard Gray 1826–1910
- Arnold
  1798–
- Ezekiel
  1801–1855
  m. Bethany Gray
  1811–1891
- William Rowan
  1800–1848
  m. Mariah Ann
  1817–1850
  (*family moved to Stumpy Point*)
  children:
  Abraham F. 1834–1891
  Elizabeth 1836–
  Edward D. 1840–
  Dorcas 1843–
  Loranzo Dowe 1845–1908
- Christian
- Loranza Dowe
  1825–1860
  m. Elizabeth Ann
  1826–
  children:
  Elizabeth 1852–
  Sabra 1862–1893
- Davis
- Elizabeth
  m. Thomas
  Scarborough
  children:
  J.P. Gray
  Zachariah
  Sarah Richard

children of Ezekiel and Bethany Gray

Cyrus King
1831–1885
m. Mary Richard Farrow
1833–1916

Isaac Littleton
1836–1873
m. Elizabeth P. Scarborough
1840–1923
children:
Isaac K. 1858–1929
Euphemia Jones 1861–1945
Mary B. 1862–1943
Elizabeth 1868–

Dilly(Delia)
1839–1882
m. Thomas Campen
1839–1902
children:
Mary 1862–1904
Benjamin 1870–1957
Alexina 1874–1879
Bethany 1877–1967
Phoebe 1879–1881

Catherine Rebecca
1846–1915
m. Sanders P. Gray
1840–1906
**see Gray pedigree chart*

Mary Ann
1850–1884
m. Tilman Day Miller
1846–1906
**see Miller pedigree chart*

Bethany
1855–1928
m. John Quidley
1853–1919

Isaac Littleton
1858–1942
m1. Sally Price
m2. Rebecca B. Miller
1871–1904

Eliza
1858–

Ezekiel B.
1860–1867

Cyrus Richard
1865–1941
m1. Bethany Gray
1871–1888
m2. Dorcas M. Scarborough
1869–1909
m3. Delphine Williams
1872–1943

Leonard S.
1866–1886

Virginia D.
1869–1886

Cora M.
1874–1894

**c. 1635 Charles Hooper was recorded as the first Hooper at Charles City (later Prince George County), VA.* Virginia Magazine *Vol. V p. 316–318*

MEEKINS

Richard Meekins
[*located in Dorchester County, Maryland in 1669*]
–1710
m1. Joanna –1699
m2. Mary

Richard Jr.
c. 1671–1718
m. Sarah

John
1674–1733
m1. Hagar Robison
m2. Mary
children: John Jr., Isaac, Thomas, James, Joseph, Mary Barnes, Elizabeth Mace, Hagar, Ann, Betty

Abraham
m. Mary

John
m. Mary

Richard
m1. Elizabeth
m2. Hannah

William
c. 1700–1775 [*Currituck County*]
m1. Elizabeth Pattison 1713–1755
m2. Elizabeth

Jacob

Roger
1747–1793
m. Elizabeth Margery

William W.
1755–1817
m. Sarah
1796–1871

Caleb

Richard

John

Moses

Mary

Jemima

Nice

children:
Elizabeth Betsy 1769–
Ann 1771–
Mary 1774–
Jeremiah 1776–1828
Lovey 1778–1830
Daniel 1781–1825
William 1784–
George 1787–
Margaret 1789–
Lemuel 1792–

William W. Meekins 1755–1817
m. Sarah 1796–1871

Silvaneous 1790–1873
m. Sarah (Sally) 1796–1871

Isaac 1780–
m. Charlotte Miller 1780–

Sally (Sarah)
m. Abraham Farrow
1793–1847

Fields (Felix)
1813–1881
m1. Mary D. Gray
1817–1851
m2. Rhoda Casey

Dameron G. 1825–
m1. Martha 1832–
m2. Larrow (Laura) Pamela Ward Stowe
children:
Martha 1852–
Manson 1858–
Anna 1862–
Sarah 1868–
Laura D. 1870 –1905
John W. 1865–1935
William C. 1876–1885 died young

Mary Polly 1817–1860
m. Thomas Williams
children:
Isaac J. 1832–1916
Josheph Silvey 1834–1893
Thomas 1844–

Louisa Douglas
1815–1889

children of Mary and Fields Meekins

Charlotte
1838–1880
2 wife of Selby Gray
1832–1882

Silvaneous
1840–1915
m Olief (Olive) Gray
1844–1924

Isaac T. 1863–1925 *m* Henrietta Scarborough 1873–1918
Andrew J. 1867–1944 *m* Mary Christian Scarborough 1872–1935
Shanklin H. 1869–1946 *m* Mary T. Barnes 1874–1966
Dorcas Delphine 1872–1943 *m* Irvin Williams 1864–1906
Sarah Jane 1874– *m* Bannister B. Price
Mary Howard 1874– *m* Warren Davis O'Neal 1869–1937
Manson 1877–1966 *m* Rhoda Ann Williams 1880–1951
Nancy H. 1885–1913 *m* Horatio S. Gray 1877–1932
Mariah 1876–

John B.
1845–1884
m Nancy Jane Gray
1850–1909
children:
George C. 1871–1935
William L. 1876–1954

Dameron Stanley
1848–1886
m1. Nancy
m2. Rhoda Scarborough
1853–1886

children of Dameron and Nancy

Howard S.
1873–1940
unmarried

Eliza Ann
1874–1953
m George Meekins
1871–1935

children of Dameron and Rhoda

Martha D.
1879–1913
m Isaac J. Williams
1862–1945

James W.
1881–

David Fields
1883–1963
m Menvil Lucretia Gray
1882–1959

child of Rhoda and Fields Meekins

Mavtisse (Mavey)
1855–1887
m Anderson Gray
1852–1908

MIDYETT/MIDGETTE

Whether it's spelled Midgett, Midgette, Midyett, or Midyette, chances are they all are descended from a shipwrecked French seaman, Matthew Midyett, tossed ashore at Chickamock Banks around 1700.
Virginian Pilot *July 1986 by Ida Kay Jordan*

Thomas Madyett/Midyett
c. 1525 [*France or England—It seems the original line came from France*]
**will of Matthew Midyett as forward for Midgett family*

Sir Henry Madyett/Midyett
1545 [*France*]–1595 [*Northolt, Middlesex, England*]
m Alice Moline 1548–1596

Joseph Midyett
1574 [*France*]–1671 [*St. Andrew, Holborn, London, England*]
m Estell Lnuk 1575–

[*children of Joseph born in France*] John 1642–, Samuel 1640–1708, Jacob 1641–, Mary 1644–
[*son of Joseph born in Kingston, Surry, England*] Thomas Midyett 1608–1663 [*died in Salisbury, Essex, Massachusetts, US*]
m Ann Woreton 1608–

Thomas Midgett 1640–1700

John Midyett 1644 [*France*]–1708 [*James City, Maryland*]
m Catherine Maggott 1635–

Matthew Midgette/Midyett 1676 [*James City, Maryland, US*]–1734 [*Bodie Island, Currituck, NC, US*]
m Judith Ann White 1681–1744
children:
Samuel Midyett Sr. 1704–1780 *m* Mary Paine 1707–1778
John Midyett 1706–1735 *m* Sarah Paine 1709–1735
Ann Midyett 1709–1732 *m* George Pugh –*c.* 1738
Joseph Midyett 1712–1771 *m* Elizabeth Margery Etheridge 1713–1775
Mathew Midyett Jr. 1715–1739 *m* Judith Paine
Catherine Midyett 1716–*circa* 1776 *m* Ezekiel Hooper *c.* 1712– *pedigree for Catherine Midyette listed in Ezekiel Hooper pedigree*
Thomas Midyett Sr. 1717–1789 *m* Bethany Bannister Farrow 1734–1795
Judith Midyett 1719–1771 *m* William Daniels *c.* 1702–
Dinah Midyett 1721–1784 *m* Thomas Morris

Matthew Midgette/Midyett
1676 [*James City, Maryland US*]–1734 [*Bodie Island, Currituck, NC, US*]
m. Judith Ann White 1681–1744

Thomas Midyett Sr
1717–1789
m. Bethany Bannister Farrow
(*daughter of Daniel and Bethany Judith Bannister Farrow*)
c. 1720–1795

- Judith 1762–1841, *m.* Maurice Baum II –1809
- Bethany 1759–1841
- Zilpah 1753–1804
- Mary 1739–1804, *m.* Thomas Paine
- Thomas Midyett Jr. 1747–1804, *m.* Lydia Parker 1755–1783
- Bannister I *c.* 1743–1804, *m.* Lauranah Jennett *c.* 1765–1838
- Daniel 1750–1810
- Dorcas 1765– *died young*
- Francis 1742–1790, *m.* Elizabeth Esther

Timothy Midgett Sr. *c.* 1770–1810 [*Currituck County*]
m. Sarah *c.* 1772–1812

- Timothy (Jr.) II 1796–1846, Rebecca Peele (*Rebecca first married Jack A. Farrow, Sr.*) *c.* 1805–
- Sarah Ann 1795–1830, *m.* Joseph Mann
- John Edward 1790–1849, *m1.* Amelia Scarborough, *m2.* Fereby
- Abner
- Frances
- Thomas 1802–

William Riley Midgett ("Alfred")
1832–1905
m. Mary Demercer Scarborough
1839–1920

children of William Riley and Mary Demercer Midgett

Sarah Ann Rebecca	John N.	Edward James	William Thomas	Peleg Willis	Evan James	Mary Williams Midgett (Gray)
1856–1933	1858–1882	1861–1944	1866–1933	1870–1949	1873–1954	1876–1954 *m.* Oliver (Obbie) James Gray 1873–1940

Matthew Midgette/Midyett
1676 [*James City, Maryland US*]–1734 [*Bodie Island, Currituck, NC, US*]
m. Judith Ann White 1681–1744

Samuel	John	Joseph	Matthew	Thomas Midyett Sr	Ann	Catherine	Judith	Dinah
				1717–1789 *m.* Bethany Bannister Farrow *(daughter of Daniel and Judith Farrow)* *c.* 1720–1795				

Judith	Bethany	Zilpah	Mary	Bannister Midyett I	Daniel Midyett	Dorcas	Francis	Thomas Midyett Jr.
1762–1841 *m.* Maurice Baum	1759–1841 *m.* George Pugh Jr.	1753–1804	1739–1804 *m.* Thomas Paine 1735–1804	*c.* 1743–1804 *m.* Lauranah Jennett *c.* 1745–1838 *daughter of Jesse and Fanny Milller Jennette*	1750–1810 *m1.* Rebecca Sparrow 1753–1798 *m2.* Elizabeth Meekins 1769–1796	1765– *died young*	1742–1790	1747–1804 *m.* Lydia Parker 1755–1783

children of Daniel and Rebecca Sparrow

- Sparrow 1775–1837
  m. Mary Watson
  2m. Rachel Berry 1811–1873
  children of Sparrow and Rachel:
  William Sylvester
  Stephen Delamar 1833–1897
  m. Emmie L.
  Little John Pugh 1835–1905
  m. Amanda E. Pegram 1834–1908
- Rebecca Sparrow
  1782–
  m. Jeremiah Meekins
  1776–
- Bannister
  1784–1828 "Little"
- Bethany
  c. 1780–1841
  m. David Paine
- Daniel Jr.
  1784–1810
- Thomas 1785–
  **Listed "in a state of insanity" in Daniels will recorded in Currituck Court 1810*

children of Daniel and Elizabeth Meekins Midyett

- Nicodemus
  1779–1844
  **Spouse Unkown*
  - Dorcas F. Midgett Scarborough 1834–*c.* 1880 *m.* Ignatious H. Scarborough 1823–1860 [*Avon*]
    children:
    Esther, Melvina, Benjamin, Jane, Comfort, Dorcas Missouri, James Walter
  - Anna W. Midgett Scarborough *c.* 1826–1856
    m. Napolean Howard 1828– 1847 Farrow 1828– *2m.* Henderson Scarborough 1827–1881 [*Avon*]
    children: Ida, Anna, Andrew, Rebecca
  - Mary Elizabeth Wallace Midyett Scarborough 1830–1897 *m.* Zion F. Scarborough 1829–1915 [*Avon*]
    children: William, Ignatious Jr., George, Zion, Jesse E., Margaret E
  - Martha M. Meekins 1832– *m.* Dameron Meekins [*Avon*]
- Anna M.
  c. 1790–1840
  m. William Weatherington
  1786–1855
  child:
  Elizabeth
- Ebenezer
  1791–
- Peggy
  1798–
- Ira Brock 1806–1870
  (1st. husband of) Spouse
  1. Mary Louisa Gray
  1809–1850
  Spouse 2. Angelico
  children of Ira and Mary Louise Gray:
  "Little" Nicodemus 1828–1901, Eorea Dameron 1829–, Arcade A. 1830–*c.* 1850, Ebenezer 1839–1905, Ira Brock Jr. 1839–1870, George Washington 1846–1871, Nathan O. 1845–1873

child of Bannister Daniel I and Lauranah Jennette

Bannister Daniel II* 1766–1824
m. Celia Pugh 1767–1839
(daughter of Thomas and Hannah Pugh)

**buried at Brooks–Midyett Cemetery, Mt. Pleasant (It has been handed down that before Bannister died, he requested to be buried "standing up" in order that he might waste no time in "seeing the face of the blessed Jesus, my Savior, on that great day of resurrection when I shall receive my soul again." When Bannister died and was interred in the Cemetery at Mount Pleasant he was "standing up" as he had asked.*

Banister Daniel III	Benjamin Harvey	Daniel 1800–1852	George Pugh	"Little" John Pugh	Celia	Bethaney	Mary Elizabeth (Polly)
1786–1844 *m.* Charlotte (Flora) Flowers 1790–1841	1792–1861 *m.* Aseneth Daniels 1796–1867 *children:* Banister Daniel 1818–1842 Mary L. 1796–1862	*m1.* Sally Erby Pugh *m2.* Bethaney Payne	1803–1842	1807–1842 *m.* Louisa *child:* Benjamin	1815–1870 *m.* James Pugh	*m.* Joshua O'Neal	1796–1862 *m.* Israel Brooks 1789– *children:* Nancy, Daniel, Israel Pat

MILLER

Thomas Miller I 1660–1720 [*Currituck Co.*]
m Unknown

Evan Miller Sr. 1690–1745
m Lina

Thomas Miller II 1720–1785
[*Moved to Frisco. First Miller to owned property on Hatteras Island*]
m Unknown

- William Bembry 1750–1805 *m* Priscilla Smith 1760–1811
  William moved to Avon
  - William –1792 *m* Mary O'Neal
    children: Frances, Uphanne
  - Phillip Allen 1792–1826 *m* *Jemia (Jennia) Stowe
    Jemia later married Noah Price Sr.
    **recorded in Benjamin Stowe Bible*
  - Elizabeth *m* Cornelious Harris
  - Charlotte 1780– *m* Isaac Meekins 1780–
  - Fanny *m* Fields O'Neal
  - Lavill
  - Euphan
  - Enoch 1788–1855 *m* Sabrey Flowers 1794–1819
- Thomas Jr.
- Mary *m* John Brooks
- Bethiah *m* Gary Clark
- Betty *m* Taylor
- Fanny *c.* 1760– *m* Jesse Jennett 1776–

child of Phillip Allen and Jemia
Frances (Fanny)
1817–
m Allen Gray
1818–
(Allen son of Ezekiel & Christian Gray)

child of Charlotte and Isaac
Sarah Sally Meekins
1820–1885
m Ervin Williams
1815–1865
**see Ervin Williams pedigree chart*

children of Enoch and Sabrey

Hezekiah Claughton
1810–1890
m Bethania Gray
1830–1891

Tilman F.
1819–1878
m Amelia H. Scarborough
1821–1881

Tilmon Day 1846–1906
m1 Mary Ann Hooper 1850–1884
children:
Christopher C. 1870–1917
m Minnie H. Midgett
Henrietta J. 1872–1900
2nd wife of: Franklin T. Gray 1865–1906
William Bembry 1875–1964
m Caroline Gray 1878–1953
Deliah (Dillie) J. Herbert 1883–1969
m Charles W. Herbert

m2 of Tilmon:
Sarah Sallie Williams 1847–1917
(1st husband of Sarah was William Scarborough)
child: Henderson S. 1885–1966
m Dorcas Price 1886–1981

Sabrah
1848–1914
m Joseph Scarborough

Miles (Willis)
1851–

William Bembry
1850–1921
m1 Nancy Scarborough
m2 Fanny W. Farrow

Bethany
1854–1885
m Washington W. Scarborough
child:
Ezekiel Scarborough
1877–1921
m Susan Austin

Ervin F.
1857–1913
m Sabra Ann Williams
1860–1906

Thomas Miller II 1720–1785
(owned property on Hatteras Island)

- William Bembry, 1750–1805, *m.* Priscilla Smith, 1760–1811
  - William, –1792, *m.* Mary O'Neal
  - Phillip Allen, 1792–1826, *m.* Jemia; *child:* Frances (Fanny)
  - Elizabeth, *m.* Cornelious Harris
  - Charlotte, 1780–, *m.* Isaac Meekins; *child:* Sarah
  - Fanny, *m.* Fields O'Neal
  - Lavill
  - Euphan
  - Enoch, 1788–1885, *m.* Sabra Flowers, 1794–1819
    - Hezekiah C.
    - Tilman R., 1819–1878, *m.* Amelia Scarborough, 1821–1881
      - Bateman P., 1841–1911, *m1.* Angeline Styron, 1844–1925, *m2.* Mary H. Gray, 1866–; *child:* Jones L., 1864–1945
      - Christopher C., 1844–1929, Emma Fulcher, 1844–1895, *m2.* Mary Ormond Tyer, 1864–1950
      - Hezekiah Claughton, 1846–1918, *m.* Esther Farrow Quidley
      - Esther, 1849–
      - Ignatious, 1849–1960
      - Harris Franklin, *m.* Ursula C. Jennette; *child:* Zeb F., 1882–1972
      - Lucinda S., 1856–
      - David Ballance, 1862–1902, *m.* Parley O'Neal; *children:* Olia, Belton, Bateman, Lillie
      - Charles F., 1859–1915, *m.* Jane"Jenny" Scarborough, 1864–1946
- Thomas Jr.
- Mary
- Bethiah
- Betty
- Fanny

Thomas Miller II 1720–1785
(owned property on Hatteras Island)

- William Bembry 1750–1805 *m.* Priscilla Smith
  - William *m.* Mary O'Neal
  - Phillip Allen *m.* Jemia; *child:* Frances (Fanny)
  - Elizabeth *m.* Cornelious Howard
  - Charlotte *m.* Isaac Meekins; *child:* Sarah
  - Fanny *m.* Fields O'Neal
  - Lavill
  - Euphan
  - Enoch 1788–1855 *m.* Sabra Flowers 1794–1819
    - Hezekiah Claughton 1810–1890 *m.* Bethania Gray 1830–1891
      - Tilmon Day 1846–1906
      - Sabra 1848–1914
        m1. Thomas Williams *(son of Evin Williams)*
        1. Joseph Mary *m.* Louisa Christian Gray *(daughter of Bannister Midgett Gray)*
        2. Noah. W.

        m2. John B. Gray *(son of Selby Gray)*
        3. David

        m3. Joseph Scarborough
        4. Polly Ann *m.* Benjamin Kelly Gray
        5. Martha *m1.* Thomas Whidbey *m2.* William Foize *m3.* Franklin Gray *(son of Malichi Gray)*
      - Miles (Willis) 1851–
      - William Bembry 1850–1921
      - Bethany 1854–1885
      - Ervin F. 1857–1913
    - Tilman F.
- Thomas Jr.
- Mary *m.* John Brooks
- Bethiah *m.* Gary Clark
- Betty *m.* Taylor
- Fanny *m.* Jesse Jennett; *child:* Lauranah *m.* Bannister Midgett

Thomas Miller II 1720–1785
[owned property on Hatteras Island]

- William Bembry 1750–1805 *m* Priscilla Smith
  - William *m* Mary O'Neal
  - Phillip Allen *m* Jemia
  - Elizabeth *m* Cornelious Howard
  - Charlotte *m* Isaac Meekins
  - Fanny *m* Fields O'Neal
  - Lavill
  - Euphan
  - Enoch 1788–1855 *m* Sabra Flowers 1794–1819
    - Hezekiah Claughton 1810–1890 *m* Bethania Gray 1830–1891
      - Tilmon Day 1846–1906
      - Sabra 1848–1914
      - Miles (Willis) 1851–
      - William Bembry 1850–1921
        m1. Nancy Scarborough
        m2. Fannie W. Farrow *(daughter of Richard Farrow)*
        children:
        1. Missouri *m1.* William Ebenezer Scarborough *m2.* Sanderson
        2. Celia R. 1884– *m* John Bunnion Quidley *(son of James I Quidley)*
        3. Dorcas Miissouri 1888–
        4. Lavina Pearl 1891–1979 *m* George Oliver O'Neal Sr.
        5. Flora B. 1894–1969 *m* Bateman Jennette
        6. Bessie 1897– *m* Roscoe Willis
      - Bethany 1854–1885
      - Ervin F. 1857–1913
    - Tilman F.
- Thomas Jr.
- Mary *m* John Brooks
- Bethiah *m* Gary Clark
- Betty *m* Taylor
- Fanny *m* Jesse Jennett

Thomas Miller II 1720–1785
[owned property on Hatteras Island]

William Bembry
1750–1805
m Priscilla Smith

Thomas Jr.

Mary
m John Brooks

Bethiah
m Gary Clark

Betty
m Taylor

Fanny
m Jesse Jennett

William
m Mary O'Neal

Phillip Allen
m Jemia

Elizabeth
m Cornelious Howard

Charlotte
m Isaac Meekins

Fanny
m Fields O'Neal

Lavill

Euphan

Enoch
1788–1855
m Sabra Flowers
1794–1819

Hezekiah Claughton 1810–1890
m Bethania Gray 1830–1891

Tilman F.

Tilmon Day
1846–1906

Sabra
1848–1914

Miles (Willis)
1851–

William Bembry
1850–1921

Bethany
1854–1885
m Washington W. Scarborough
1852–1885 *(son of Ezekial H. Scarborough)*

children:

1. Dorcas Rosa 1873–
2. Ezekiel Littleton 1876–1921
3. Cilioven (Salome) 1880–

**Bethaney and Washington were struck by lightning while in bed. Son was in the middle of bed but survived.*
(Some records state Salome was child in middle that survived)

Ervin F.
1857–1913

Thomas Miller II 1720–1785
[*owned property on Hatteras Island*]

- William Bembry 1750–1805 *m* Priscilla Smith
  - William *m* Mary O'Neal
  - Phillip Allen *m* Jemia
  - Elizabeth *m* Cornelious Howard
  - Charlotte *m* Isaac Meekins
  - Fanny *m* Fields O'Neal
  - Lavill
  - Euphan
  - Enoch 1788–1855 *m* Sabra Flowers 1794–1819
    - Hezekiah Claughton 1810–1890 *m* Bethania Gray 1830–1891
      - Tilmon Day 1846–1906
      - Sabra 1848–1914
      - Miles (Willis) 1851–
      - William Bembry 1850–1921
      - Bethany 1854–1885
      - Ervin F. 1857–1913 *m* Sabra Ann Williams (*daughter of Isaac James Williams*)

        children:
        1. Nancy Jane 1880– *m* John Alfred Farrow (*John son of John Pharoah Farrow*)
        2. Mary Wilson 1886– *m* William Ebenezer Scarborough
        3. Evangeline Willie 1889– *m* Harris Edgar Miller
    - Tilman F.
- Thomas Jr.
- Mary *m* John Brooks
- Bethiah *m* Gary Clark
- Betty *m* Taylor
- Fanny *m* Jesse Jennett

Thomas Miller II 1720–1785
[*owned property on Hatteras Island*]

- William Bembry 1750–1805 *m* Priscilla Smith
  - William *m* Mary O'Neal
  - Phillip Allen *m* Jemia
  - Elizabeth *m* Cornelious Howard
  - Charlotte *m* Isaac Meekins
  - Fanny *m* Fields O'Neal
  - Lavill
  - Euphan
  - Enoch 1788–1855 *m* Sabra Flowers 1794–1819
    - Hezekiah
    - Tilman F. 1819–1878 *m* Amelia Scarborough 1821–1881
      - Bateman P. 1841–1911
      - Christopher C. 1844–1929
        m1. Emma Dolly Fulcher
        1. Henderson Seymor 1870–1917 *m* Mollie Toler
        2. Baxter B. 1871–1949 *m* Josephine Drinkwater Gray
        3. Lorena E. 1873–1902 *m* George Fulcher
        4. Odessie *m* Luther Fulcher
        5. Amelia T. 1875–1881
        6. Lilly C. *m* Thomas Baum 1877–1938
        7. Delphin 1878–1966
        8. Permelia *m* 1888–1889

        m2. Mary (Maude) Ormand Tyer 1864–1950
        9. Maude *m* Estus Prestin White 1900–1987
        10. Lucy 1898–1991 *m* Paul Parker
        11. Louise 1889–1941 *m* Meekins
        12. Annie *m* Hodges
      - Hezekiah Claughton
      - Esther 1849–
      - Ignatious 1849–1960
      - Harris Franklin 1852–1931
      - Lucinda S. 1856–
      - David Ballance 1862–1902
      - Charles F. 1859–1915
- Thomas Jr.
- Mary *m* John Brooks
- Bethiah *m* Gary Clark
- Betty *m* Taylor
- Fanny *m* Jesse Jennett

Thomas Miller II 1720–1785
[*owned property on Hatteras Island*]

William Bembry 1750–1805 *m.* Priscilla Smith
Thomas Jr.
Mary *m.* John Brooks
Bethiah *m.* Gary Clark
Betty *m.* Taylor
Fanny *m.* Jesse Jennett

Children of William Bembry:

William *m.* Mary O'Neal
Phillip Allen *m.* Jemia
Elizabeth *m.* Cornelious Howard
Charlotte *m.* Isaac Meekins
Fanny *m.* Fields O'Neal
Lavill
Euphan
Enoch 1788–1855 *m.* Sabra Flowers 1794–1819

Children of Enoch:

Hezekiah
Tilman F. 1819–1878 *m.* Amelia Scarborough 1821–1881

Children of Tilman F.:

Bateman P. 1841–1911
Christopher C. 1844–1929
Hezekiah Claughton 1846–1918
m. Esther Farrow Quidley
(daughter of John Quidley)
children:
1. Rebecca B.
2. Annie T. 1873– *m.* Jarvis Seely
3. Franklin McCarter 1875–1953
4. Charles 1877–
5. Mary Washington
6. David Milville 1886–

Esther 1849–
Ignatious 1849–1960
Harris Franklin 1852–1931
Lucinda S. 1856–
David Ballance 1862–1902
Charles F. 1859–1915

Thomas Miller II 1720–1785
[owned property on Hatteras Island]

- William Bembry 1750–1805 *m* Priscilla Smith
  - William *m* Mary O'Neal
  - Phillip Allen *m* Jemia
  - Elizabeth *m* Cornelious Howard
  - Charlotte *m* Isaac Meekins
  - Fanny *m* Fields O'Neal
  - Lavill
  - Euphan
  - Enoch 1788–1855 *m* Sabra Flowers 1794–1819
    - Hezekiah
    - Tilman F. 1819–1878 *m* Amelia Scarborough 1821–1881
      - Bateman P. 1841–1911
      - Christopher C. 1844–1929
      - Hezekiah Claughton 1846–1918
      - Esther 1849–
      - Ignatious 1849–1960
      - Harris Franklin 1852–1931 *m* Ursula C. Jennette *(Daughter of Wallace Jennette)*
        children:
        1. Fraizer 1877– *m* Cora Gray *(daughter of Malachi Gray)*
        2. Fredrick 1880–
        3. Zeblon 1882–
        4. Edgar 1886– *m* Evangeline Willie Miller
        5. Erskin 1890–
        6. Alston 1893–
      - Lucinda S. 1856–
      - David B. 1862–1902
      - Charles F. 1859–1915
- Thomas Jr.
- Mary *m* John Brooks
- Bethiah *m* Gary Clark
- Betty *m* Taylor
- Fanny *m* Jesse Jennett

Thomas Miller II 1720–1785
[owned property on Hatteras Island]

- William Bembry 1750–1805 *m* Priscilla Smith
  - William *m* Mary O'Neal
  - Phillip Allen *m* Jemia
  - Elizabeth *m* Cornelious Howard
  - Charlotte *m* Isaac Meekins
  - Fanny *m* Fields O'Neal
  - Lavill
  - Euphan
  - Enoch 1788–1855 *m* Sabra Flowers 1794–1819
    - Hezekiah
    - Tilman F. 1819–1878 *m* Amelia Scarborough 1821–1881
      - Bateman P. 1841–1911
      - Christopher C. 1844–1929
      - Hezekiah Claughton 1846–1918
      - Esther 1849–
      - Ignatious 1849–1960
      - Harris Franklin 1852–1931
      - Lucinda S. 1856–
      - David B. 1862–1902
      - Charles F. 1859–1915 *m* Jane (Jenny) Scarborough *(daughter of Ignatious Scarborough)* *children:*
        1. Clarence W. 1888–
        2. Inez 1891– *m* Caleb Lincoln
        3. Ralph 1903–1905 *died young*
- Thomas Jr.
- Mary *m* John Brooks
- Bethiah *m* Gary Clark
- Betty *m* Taylor
- Fanny *m* Jesse Jennett

PRICE

Thomas Price *c.* 1640–1691
m. Unknown

Mary | Rebecca | Ann | Thomas Price II | Edward | Margaret | Elizabeth

Thomas Price II
c. 1670–
(Elizabeth City County, VA currently Hampton VA)
m. Rachael Hern

William Price *c.* 1698–1740
m. Elizabeth Godwin 1705–

Jacob Price 1730–*c.* 1790
Nansemond County, VA
m. Unknown

Henry Price *c.* 1755–1806
**First Price to move to Hatteras Island, NC (present day Avon) between 1786–1790*
m. Nancy Scarborough *c.* 1755–1815

Noah Price Sr. (I) *c.*1787–1860
m.1. Elizabeth Williams 1785–1860
(father–Asa Williams)
m.2. Jemia *c.* 1794–
(previously married to Phillip Miller 1792–1826)

Noah Price Sr. (I)
*c.*1787–1860
m1. Elizabeth Williams
1785–1860
m2. Jemia
c. 1794–

children of Noah and Elizabeth

Cynthia 1828–1917
m. Wallace Gray
1822–1899
(son of Ezekiel & Christian Williams Gray)

Tilmon J. Gray 1859–1897
m. Lucinda J.Farrow 1855–1950

Willie Ann Gray 1878–1954
m. John Devine Farrow 1875–1934
children:
Emma, Dorcas, Lucy

Bateman 1820–1891
m1. Elizabeth Farrow
m2. Brittana Farrow 1828–
m3. Margaret Williams
1840–1917

Noah Price Jr (II)
1834–1882
m1. Dorcas B. Gray
1833–1864
m2. Malissa F. Morgan

children of Noah Price Jr. and Dorcas Gray
1. Colinda (Landa) 1861–1940 *m1.* Ezekiel Scarborough *m2.* and *3rd. wife of* Ignatious Scarborough *m3.* Oliver O'Neal Midgett 1865–1934
2. Amblick Thomas 1864–1940 *m.* Delilah Elizabeth (Dillie) O'Neal

children of Noah Price Jr. and Malissa F. Morgan
3. Banister Boyd 1868–1956 *m.* Sarah Jane Meekins 1874–1949
4. Shepherd Wilson 1872– *m.* Comfort Gray 1877–1939
5. Erastus *died young*

Tilmon 1837–
m. Elizabeth
Scarborough

Holloway 1818–1870
m. Cordelia
Scarborough 1823–

Noah Price Sr. (I) *c.*1787–1860
m.1. Elizabeth Williams 1785–1860
m.2. Jemia *c.* 1794

children of Noah and Elizabeth

Cynthia 1828–1917
m. Wallace Gray
1822–1899

Bateman 1820–1891
m1. Elizabeth Farrow
m2. Brittana Farrow 1828–
m3. Margaret Williams
1840–1917

Noah Price Jr (II)
1834–1882
m1. Dorcas B. Gray
1833–1864
m2. Malissa F. Morgan

Tilmon 1837–
m. Elizabeth
Scarborough

Holloway 1818–1870
m. Cordelia
Scarborough 1823–

child of Noah Price Jr. and Dorcas Gray
Amblick Thomas 1864–1940
m. Delilah Elizabeth (Dillie) O'Neal 1865–1934

Dorcas Ann 1886–1981 *m.* Henderson Stanley Miller 1885–1966
Ellevy 1888–1909
Elva *m.* Sam Smith [*Milan, GA*]
Celia 1890–
Lillian 1891 *died young*
Lutishia (Tish) Christian 1892–1967 *2nd wife of:* Isaac Stanley Williams 1887–1935
Noah Ervin 1895–1971 *m.* Salome Barnes Meekins 1897–1984
Margaret 1898– *died young*
Pecola 1900–1987 *m.* Dorther James Gray 1883–1966
Amblick Jr. 1903–1956
Elizabeth 1905–1992 *m1.* Arthur Stowe 1889–1975 *m2.* and *2nd. spouse of Edward Franklin Williams 1901–1982 (no children)*
Lizzie 1905– *m.* Lorenzo Hooper 1869–1944
Alevina 1910–

Noah Price Sr. (I) *c.*1787–1860
m1. Elizabeth Williams 1785–1860
m2. Jemia *c.* 1794

children of Noah and Elizabeth

Cynthia 1828–1917
m. Wallace Gray
1822–1899

Bateman 1820–1891
m1. Elizabeth Farrow
m2. Brittana Farrow 1828–
m3. Margaret Williams
1840–1917

Noah Price Jr (II)
1834–1882
m1. Dorcas B. Gray
1833–1864
m2. Malissa F. Morgan

Tilmon 1837–
m. Elizabeth
Scarborough

Holloway 1818–1870
m. Cordelia
Scarborough 1823–

children of Noah Price Jr. and Malissa Morgan

Sheppherd Wilson b. 1872
m. Comfort 1877–1939

Amblick Thomas 1864–1940
m. Delilah Elizabeth (Dillie) O'Neal
1865–1934

Noah Ervin Price 1895–1971
m. Salome Barnes Meekins 1897–1984
(daughter of Shanklin Meekins)

Ervin H. 1917–1977 *m.* Ernestine Whidbee 1921–2004
Alvan T. *m.* Doris Cole
Hubert G. *m.* Mary Christine (Chris) Jones
Herman *m.* Mamie Dean
Noah H. 1927–1991 *m.* Rose O'Neal 1936–1994
Juan Baynard 1930–2007 *unmarried*
Meschil Belle 1931–2013 *m.* Preston Quidley 1924–1986

Banister B. 1868–1956
m. Sarah Jane Meekins 1874–1949
children:
Alvin 1899–1981
Selby Underwood 1904–1925

Portions of the information for the Price genealogy was taken from the Collection of Ancestral Research by Hubert G. Price (son of Noah Ervin Price).

Noah Price Sr. (I) *c.*1787–1860
m1. Elizabeth Williams 1785–1860
m2. Jemia *c.* 1794

children of Noah and Elizabeth

Cynthia 1828–1917
m. Wallace Gray
1822–1899

Bateman 1820–1891
m1. Elizabeth Farrow
m2. Brittana Farrow 1828–
m3. Margaret Williams
1840–1917

Noah Price Jr (II)
1834–1882
m1. Dorcas B. Gray
1833–1864
m2. Malissa F. Morgan

Tilmon 1837–
m. Elizabeth
Scarborough

Holloway 1818–1870
m. Cordelia
Scarborough 1823–

Hulda Ann 1844–1913
m. Robert Watson Gray
1837–1913

Edward 1846–1908
m. Mary "Polly" Smith
1856–

Roann H
1849–

Brittany 1856
m. and second wife of: David O'Neal

Cordelia 1866–1955
m. Anderson L. Gray
1852–1908

Rhoades

Oliver (Obbie) J.
1873–1940
m. Mary Williams Midgett
1876–1954

Hosania
1862–1863
died young

David Watson
1865–1866
died young

Polly Ann
1866–1885
m. Thomas Gray
1856–1921

George M.
1869–1918
m. Montra Meekins
1870–1949

Bethany B.
1871–1888
m. and first wife of:
Cyrus Richard Hooper
1865–1941

Bateman W.
1875–1885
died young

Willard James Gray 1894–1969 *m1.* Eunice Hooper Gray 1893–1967 *m2.* Beatrice Hogan *c.* 1895–1988
Lovie Ann Gray Gray 1897–1944 *2nd. S of:* Eugene Grandberry Gray 1889–1966
Lillian P. Gray 1899–1984 *m.* Bateman P. Miller 1876–
Ellis Andrew Gray 1902–1989 *m.* Caroline Rowland Gray 1914–2005
Amanda Gray Gray 1907–1985 *m.* Burgess Anderson Gray 1902–1988
Amelia Gray 1907–1908 *died young*
Oliver (Obbie) James Gray Jr. 1904–1978 *m.* Christine Williams 1906–1982
Robert Watson Gray 1908–1989 *m.* Isabella Williams Scarborough 1911–1959
Edward S. 1910–1911 *died young*
Cyril M. Gray 1914–1980 *m.* Grace Gray 1914–1992
John "Jack" Berchman 1927–1997 *m.* Anna Scarborogh 1934–2011 *(John son of Willard J. and Beatrice Hogan Gray, raised by Oliver and Mary Gray)*

SCARBOROUGH

According to Hubert Price, Edmund Scarborough was the first Scarborough that migrated from North Walsham, England and settled in Accomac County (Eastern Shore, Va.) on Midgett Bay in 1635. Edmund was sheriff of Northhampton Co., Va. in 1661. He was also a member of House of Burgess from Accomac. He had two sons Charles and George. George's family later moved to Pasquatank Co., NC. The Scarborough's of Avon came from this line.

George Scarborough
Pasquotank—near North River 1714 Tax List.
Family later moved to Avon.

Austin (Augustus) Scarborough

*Nancy
c. 1755–1815
m. Henry Price
1755–1840
**Nancy pedigree listed under Price pedigree*

George
c. 1792–
m. Sarah Scarborough
1797–

Edward
–1801

William E. Scarborough
1764–1824
m. Christian Farrow
1797–1846
(daughter of Pharoah Farrow)

Ignatious
1750–1801
m. Keziah
1750–1800
(daughter of Keziah and James Williams)
Keziah–Hebrew name Cassia means sweet scented spice–Daughter of Job in the Bible.

Fanny

Children of William E. Scarborough and Christian Farrow:

Banister
1817–1890
m1. Dollie Casey
m2. Esther F.
1832–1905

John
1826–
m. Malisa Farrow
1824–

Stancil Scarborough
1812–1874
m. Rosetta Rosemond Farrow
1820–1880

Pharoah Farrow S.
1829–
m1. Eliza
m2. Francis Farrow

* Elizabeth Jane
1836–1870
m. "Little" Anderson Gray
1832–1905
**Elizabeth pedigree listed under Gray pedigree*

children of Stancil and Rosetta Scarborough

Brittania
1844–1876
m. Bannister B.Gray
1842–1916

William Ebenezer
1847–1871
m. Sarah Sally Wil-
liams
1847–1917

Sarah
1850–
died young

Farrow Langford
Scarborough
1854–1926
m. Melvina Pegram
Scarborough
1861–1946

Mary Christian
1850–1929
m. Merchant Gideon
Williams
1844–1917

Amy
1857–
died young

Celestial
Sumner
1885–1968
m. Sudie Peele
1894–1980

Arkansas
1892–1960
m. Ulysses W.
Hooper
1890–1977

Dewey Hobson
1898–1964
m. Katherine Wil-
liams
1896–1991

Edward Farrow
“Fair”
1883–1973
m1. Rebecca
Wallace Williams
1883–1916
m2. Addie J. Gray
1918–1973

Erskine
“Blucher”
1890–1967
m. Beulah Gray
1897–1974

Ignatious
Grandy
1902–1998
m. Leona Wil-
liams
1907–1970

Walker Blaine
1895–1993
m. Edna Midgett
1906–1989

Betty”Teeny”
Isabella
1881–1964
m. Dameron
Nelson Gray
1883–1960

Lillian B.
1887–1917
m. James E. Wil-
liams
1882–1937

George Scarborough *near North River*

Austin (Augustus) Scarborough

- *Nancy, *c.* 1755–1815, *m.* Henry Price 1755–1840
- George, *c.* 1792–, *m.* Sarah Scarborough 1797–
  - Ignatious Scarborough 1823–1860, *m1.* Esther Farrow 1826–, *m2.* Dorcas F. Midyett 1834–1880
    - *children of Ignatious and Dorcas*
      - Esther Annie, 1856–1928, *m.* Patrick Etheridge 1851–1920
      - Melvina Pegram, 1861–1946, *m.* Farrow Langford Scarborough 1854–1926
      - Benjamine, 1858–, *died young*
      - Jane "Jenny", 1864–1946, *m.* Charles F. Miller 1859–1915
      - Comfort E., 1865–
      - Dorcas (Duck) Missouri, 1868–1909, *2nd wife of* Cyrus Richard Hooper 1865–1941
      - James Walter, 1872–1923, *m1.* Mary Price 1851–, *m2.* Elmetta Gray 1887–1983
  - Elizabeth 1833–, *living with Ignatious in the 1850 census*
  - Isaac 1835–, *living with Ignatious in the 1850 census*
- Edward, –1801
- William E. Scarborough, 1764–1824, *m.* Christian Farrow 1797–1846
- Ignatious, 1750–1801, *m.* Keziah 1750–1800
- Fanny

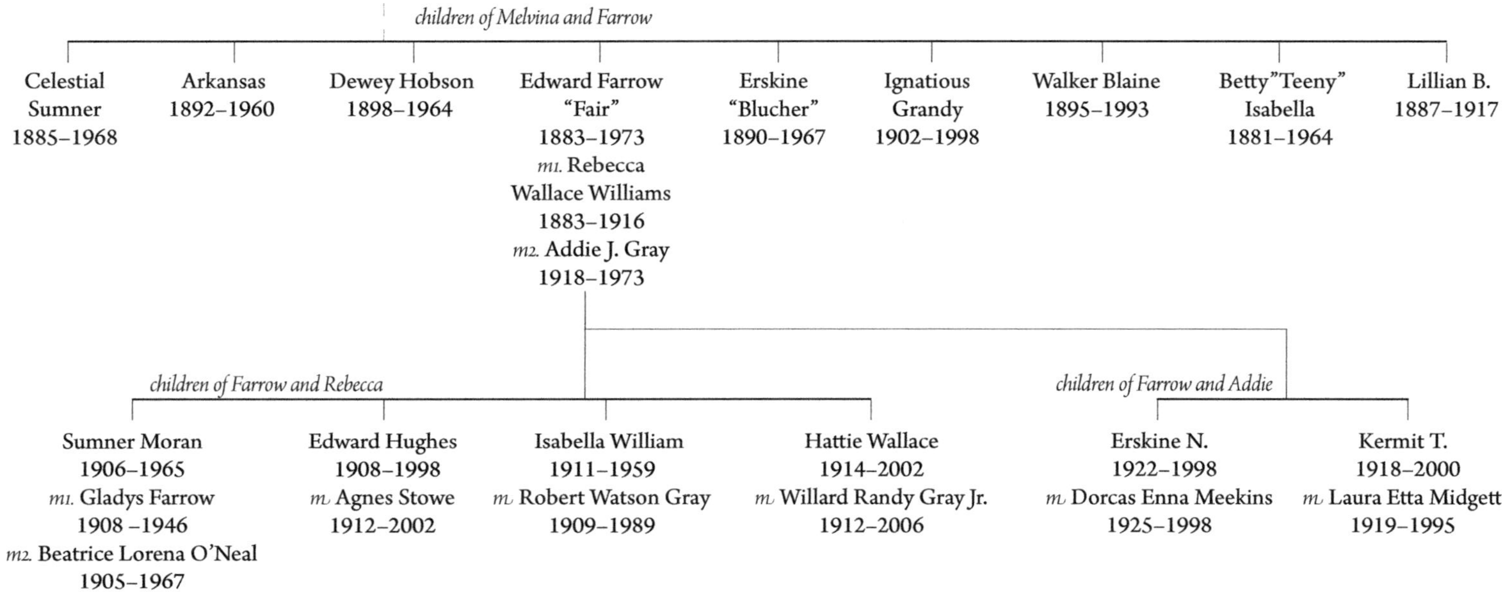
children of Melvina and Farrow
Celestial Sumner 1885–1968
Arkansas 1892–1960
Dewey Hobson 1898–1964
Edward Farrow "Fair" 1883–1973
m1. Rebecca Wallace Williams 1883–1916
m2. Addie J. Gray 1918–1973
Erskine "Blucher" 1890–1967
Ignatious Grandy 1902–1998
Walker Blaine 1895–1993
Betty"Teeny" Isabella 1881–1964
Lillian B. 1887–1917
children of Farrow and Rebecca
Sumner Moran 1906–1965
m1. Gladys Farrow 1908 –1946
m2. Beatrice Lorena O'Neal 1905–1967
Edward Hughes 1908–1998
m. Agnes Stowe 1912–2002
Isabella William 1911–1959
m. Robert Watson Gray 1909–1989
Hattie Wallace 1914–2002
m. Willard Randy Gray Jr. 1912–2006
children of Farrow and Addie
Erskine N. 1922–1998
m. Dorcas Enna Meekins 1925–1998
Kermit T. 1918–2000
m. Laura Etta Midgett 1919–1995

George Scarborough *near North River*

Austin (Augustus) Scarborough

- *Nancy
  c. 1755–1815
  m. Henry Price
  1733–1840
  ** Price pedigree chart*
- George
  c. 1792–
  m. Sarah Scarborough
  1797
- Edward
  –1801
- William E. Scarborough
  1764–1824
  m. Christian Farrow
  1797–1846
- Ignatious
  1750–1801
  m. Keziah
  1750–1800
- Fanny

Children of Ignatious and Keziah:

- Thomas 1794–1881
  m. Sarah 1798–
- Zebedee 1780–
  (some records states Ezekiel)
  m. Sally
- Bateman 1796–1860
  m. Mary Morgan 1804–1855
- Ignatious Jr.
  1780–1800

Children of Bateman and Mary Morgan:

- Henderson S.
  1827–1881
  m. Anna W. Midgett
  1826–1860
- *Amelia "Millie"
  1821–1881
  m. Tilman F. Miller
  1819–1878
  **Miller pedigree chart*
- John A. 1833–1887
  m1. Christian Meekins 1836–
  m2. Amelia Quidley 1846–
  m3. Mary Farrow
- Margaret Louisa
  1835–1880
  m. Joseph Silvey Williams
  1839–1887
- Euphemia Christian
  1839–1891
  m. Evan Garland Williams
  1837–1877
- Elizabeth "Betty" Jane
  1844–1923
  m. Isaac L. Hooper
  1836–1873

Henderson S.:

m1. Anna W. Midgett 1826–1868 *(Anna was first wife of Napolian Howard Farrow 1828–1847—son of Pharoah Farrow, her second husband was Henderson)*
children: Bateman 1851–1883, Britannia 1855–1886
m2. Harriet D. Hooper
children: Rebecca W. 1857–1922 Anna Mariah 1859–1934
m3. Mary Ann Peel
children: George M. 1869–1903, Henrietta 1872–1918
m4. Asenith Scarborough 1851–1880
child: Leah C. 1877–
m5. Lois Mann 1853–1884
child: Charles 1882–1955

George Scarborough *near North River*

- Austin (Augustus) Scarborough
  - *Nancy *c.* 1755–1815
  - George *c.* 1792–
  - Edward –1801
  - William E. Scarborough 1764–1824
  - Ignatious 1750–1801 *m.* Keziah 1750–1800
    - Thomas 1794–1881
    - Zebedee 1780–
    - Bateman 1796–1860 *m.* Mary Morgan 1804–1855
      - Henderson S. 1827–1881 *m.* Anna W. Midgett 1826–1860
      - *Amelia “Millie” 1821–1881 *m.* Tilman F. Miller 1819–1878 (**Miller pedigree chart*)
      - John A. 1833–1887 *m1.* Christian Meekins 1836– *m2.* Amelia Quidley 1846– *m3.* Mary Farrow
        - *m1.* Christian Meekins *children:* Melville 1867–1887 *m.* Eulalia Jennette 1869–1936; *m2.* Amelia; *m3.* Mary D. Farrow *child:* Randolph; *m4.* Alethia Midgett 1880–1952
      - Margaret Louisa 1835–1880 *m.* Joseph Silvey William 1839–1887
        - *children:* Thomas Litchfield, Isaac James, Margaret, Mary J., Chafter B., Clarissa A.
      - Euphemia Christian 1839–1891 *m.* Evan Garland Williams 1837–1877
        - *children:* Dorcas J., James D., Wesley Collins, Charles T.
      - Elizabeth “Betty” Jane 1844–1923 *m.* Isaac L. Hooper 1836–1873 *children:* Isaac King, Euphemia J., Mary Bateman; *m2.* Anderson Gray 1832–1905 *child:* Joshue Gibbs
    - Ignatious Jr. 1780–1800
  - Fanny

George Scarborough *near North River*

Austin (Augustus) Scarborough

*Nancy *c.* 1755–1815

George *c.* 1792–

Edward –1801

William E. Scarborough 1764–1824

Ignatious 1750–1801 *m.* Keziah 1750–1800

Fanny

Thomas 1794–1881 *m.* Sarah Gray 1798–

Zebedee 1780–

Bateman 1796–1860

Ignatious Jr. 1780–1800

Thomas 1825– *m.* Elizabeth 1827– *children:* Mary 1848–, Hulda 1851–, Sarah 1855–1939, Henry 1858–

John 1826–

Arnold 1829–1874 *m.* Julia Gray 1825–1904

Richard 1833–1900 *m1.* Sarah Sally Gray 1835–1880 *children:* Arnold 1855–, Susan 1857–1880, Nathan 1864–1929, Richard Blivens 1869–1943 *m2.* Rebecca Midgett *c.* 1856– *children:* Minnie I. 1883–1954, Sudie Jane 1890–1960

Asenith 1852–1880 *4th Spouse of:* Henderson Sarborough 1827–1881

Leah 1877– *m.* Cyrus H. Farrow 1864–

Rhoda Arnel 1858 –1886 *m.* Dameron Meekins 1848–1886

Martha D. Meekins 1879–1913 *m.* Isaac J. Williams

James W. Meekins 1881–

David Fields Meekins 1883–1963 *m.* Menvil L. Gray 1882–1959

Ezekiel 1858–1890 *m.* Colenda Price 1861–1940

Orestus 1883–1911 *m.* Mary Ervin Scarborough 1886–1916

Alziria 1903–1990

Allen McCray 1906–

Robert Washington 1909–

*William Scarborough 1797– *c.* 1880
m. Sarah (Sally) Flowers 1806–1882
**Previous genealogy on William Scarborough unknown.*

William 1828–
m. Nancy 1828–

John B. 1832–
m. Christine Meekins

Zion F. 1829–1915
m1. Mary Elizabeth Wallace Midgett 1830–1897
m2. Susan Dunn (*first married to Joseph Lewis*)

Elizabeth 1836–
m. Tillman Price 1837–

Phebe 1838–

children of Zion and Mary Scarborough:

William James Scarborough 1849–1874	*m.* Sarah Williams 1847–1917
Mary Zion Scarborough 1851–1927	*m.* James Ignatious Quidley 1844–1913 (*Mary was second wife of James*)
Dorcas Ann Scarborough 1852–1891	*m1.* Joseph Curtis Gray 1840–1877 *m2.* Benjamin Davis Scarborough
Sarah Scarborough 1854–1862 *died young*	
Ignatious H. Scarborough 1856–1923	*m1.* Dorcas Thomas Gray 1862–1942
Rebecca Scarborough 1858–1876	*m.* Jabez Jennett
George Leftis Scarborough 1861–1926	*m.* Sabra Hooper 1862–1893
Rhoda J. 1865–1865 *died young*	
Zion Bunyan Scarborough 1866–1918	*m.* Francis "Frankie" Austion 1870–1957
Margaret Etheridge Scarborough 1871–1943 (*twins*)	*m.* Ignatious M. Gray 1869–1924
Jessie E. Scarborough 1871–1899 (*twins*)	*m.* Josephine Gray 1879–1956 (*Josephine later married Andrew D. Williams*)

children of Ignatious H. Scarborough and Dorcas Thomas Gray:

Estelle Maye Scarborough 1883–1955	*m.* William Mounfield 1878–
Maude S. Scarborough 1885–1913	*m.* William R. Gray
Sarah Elizabeth Scarborough 1888–1957	*m.* Harry Burgess
Ignatious H. Scarborough Jr. 1891–1973	*m.* Izetta Matilda Gaskill 1895–1985 (*Wanchese*)
Robert Edward Scarborough 1894–1966	*m.* Mary Magdalene Tillett 1898–1974
Zebulon Vance Scarborough	*m.* Margaret Myers

WILLIAMS

William Williams 1635–1725 *m.* Mary
Sons: Thomas, Stephen, Tulle *Daughters:* Jane Brent, Abigail Phillips

Thomas Williams 1670–1732 *m.* Mary
Sons: Samuel and Joseph *Daughter:* Mary

Joseph Williams 1705–1775
(Purchased a Colonial Land Grant in the Kinnakeet Vicinity)
m. Comfort Farrow 1740–1783 *(daughter of Jacob & Amy Farrow)*

Caleb
1760–
m. Sarah

Joseph Jr.
–1821
m. Amey

Jacob
m. Rachel
Wahab

Ervin Hooper Ormand Williams
1815–1865
m. Sarah "Sally" Meekins
1820–1885

Andrew Peel Williams
1810–1868
m. Christian Flowers
1818–1856

James
m. Keziah
(daughter Keziah married Ignatious Scarborough)

Robert
m. Unknown

Asa
daughter 1 of Asa:
Elizabeth Williams
1785–1860
m1. James Scarborough
m2. Noah Price Sr.
1787–1860
daughter 2 of Asa:
Mary
m. John Gray

children of Andrew and Christian and their descendants

Evan Garland
1837–1877
m. Euphemia Christian
Scarborough
1839–1891

Zion
1856–1881

Margaret
1840–1917
3rd wife of
Bateman Price
1820–1891

- Rev. Andrew W.
  Price 1862–1937
  m. Rebecca W.
  Scarborough
  1857–1922

Franklin Pearce
1852–1856
died young

Sarah Sally
1847–1917
m1. William J. Scarborough
1849–1874
m2. Tilmon Day Miller
1846–1906

- Henderson Stanley Miller
  1885–1966
  m. Dorcas Ann Price Miller
  1886 –1981
    - Madge Miller
    - Henderson Miller

Ervin Hooper
1850–1919
m1. Brittania1855–1886
m2. Anna H. Gray
m3. Nancy Jane Gray
m4. Mary W. Gray

children of Ervin and Brittania Scarborough Williams and their descendants

Ida Williams 1874–1898
m. William W. Gray
1874–1948 (*died Ashville, NC*)

- Rora Gray

Anna Stanley Williams
1876–1943
m. Peleg W. Midgett
1870–1949

- Peleg Jr.
- Ervin
- Edith Midgett
- Becky Walker
- Dorothy Kruppa
- Edward R.
- Mary Gard

Andrew Peel Williams
1880–1951
m. Minerva W. Gray
1884–1951

- Alton Tilmon
- Helen Whitehurst
- Evelyn Lucinda
- Mildred Gray
- Jeanie Ellis
- Herschal Peele

Rebecca Wallace Williams
1883–1919
1st. wife of: Edward F. Scarborough
1883–1973

- Sumner Moran
- Edward Hughes
- Isabella Williams
- Hattie Wallace

children of Ervin Hooper Ormand Williams (son of Jacob and Rachel Wahab) and Sarah "Sally" Meekins and their descendants

Charlotte (Charity) Ann
1838–1919
m. W arren Davis O'Neal Sr.
1836–1883

Gideon C. Merchant O'Neal
1816–1923
Delilah(Dillie)
Elizabeth O'Neal
1865–1934
Mary Thomas O'Neal
1866–1948
Warren Davis O'Neal
1869–1937
Ulysses Grant O'Neal
1871–1949
Malissa G. O'Neal
1872–
Tilmon S. O'Neal
1873–1877
Joseph King O'Neal
1876–1964
Charles P. O'Neal
1879–1886
Rizzie P. O'Neal
1862–

Achsah Ann (Axy)
1840–1901
2nd. wife of:
Isaac James Williams
1834–1916

Marchant J. Williams
1862–
Ervin Hooper Williams
1864–1906
Thomas James Williams
1866–1935
Ulysess S.G. Williams
1871–
Sally Ann Williams
1874–1952
Polly F. Williams
1876–1903
Samual S. Williams
1877–1908
David King Williams
1879–1916
Ella H. Williams
1882–1904

Marchant Gideon
1844–1917
m. Mary
Christian Scarborough
1850–1929

George Wesley Williams
1872–1922
Edmond B. Williams
1876–1943
Farrow L. Williams
1880–
Brittania Williams Gray
1882–1958
Melvina Rebecca
1884–1963
Roseamond (Rosa) Williams
1886–1854
Rebecca
1886–
Sarah Sadie Williams
1892–

Sarah
1850–1877
2nd. wife of
William Benjamin
Nixon
1851–1935

Minnie D. Nixon
1875–
Neta M. Nixon
1877–

Isaac M
1853–1911
m. Dorcas M. Gray
1852–1931

Franklin Pierce Williams
1876–1951
Rhoda Ann Williams
1880–1951
James Emerite Williams
1882–1937
Andrew (Drew) David
Williams
1885–1945
Isaac Stanley Williams
1887–1935

Mary Polly
1856–
m. Edward Price
1844–1908

Holloway J Price
1873–

children of Evan Garland Williams (son of Andrew Peel and Christian Flowers) and Euphemia Christian Scarborough

Dorcas J. Williams Scarborough
1858–1926
2nd wife of Benjamin Davis Scarborough
1860–1917

Mary Ervin 1886–1916
(*m3 of* James Washington)
James Washington 1894–1976
m1. Aletha Austin of James Washington
m2. Gladys Jennette

James D. Williams
1861–1881
unmarried

Wesley Collins Williams
1872–1920
m. Hulda Ann Farrow Williams
1871–1951

Annie C. Williams
Selina Williams Gray
Claude T. Williams
Edward F. Williams
Percy D. Williams

Charles Thomas Williams
1865–1941
m. Sally Ann Williams Williams
1874–1952

Charles Thomas Williams II
Ida Pearce Williams O'Neal
Elliott Jasper Williams
Evan G. Williams
Achash V. Williams Brothers
Christian Williams Gray
Vetter Jennings Williams
Benjamin D. Williams

GOD'S MIRACULOUS WORKS

THE LIGHT

We know God is with us in the good times, but what happens when bad times occur? Is this you, God? Where are you, God? Why me, God? Paul tells us in Romans 5:3–4, "Suffering produces endurance, and, endurance produces character, and character produces hope."

But you see, God, I have been faithful to you and I have served you. Isn't Paul referring to someone who has ridiculed you or persecuted you, or has lived a wicked life?

In August 2004, I looked in the mirror and saw someone I didn't recognize. I was red as a lobster, then the swelling and itching started. A quick trip to the medical center and swift treatment by a physician, and slowly my symptoms subsided. An appointment was made with an allergist, and treatment was started. Several months later in the middle of the night, the same thing happened, but even more severe. A call by my husband to 911 resulted in more treatment and a suggestion by the EMT that I go to the hospital. We live on an island on the Outer Banks of North Carolina, and the hospital is approximately a 45-minute drive. I decided I was going to be fine and refused to go.

The next time the EMTs were called, I didn't have a choice in the matter. In addition to my previous symptoms, I passed out. God had to shut my mouth because I couldn't do it myself. In and out of consciousness, I barely remember the 45-minute trip to the hospital. In the middle of the night as I lay in a bed in the emergency room, my husband unraveled the events that led to this unanticipated visit. My attending physician was Dr. Lois. I found it unusual that this doctor and I would share the same name. This was the beginning of many unusual things that would happen. As Dr. Lois listened to my symptoms, the diagnosis casually rolled off his tongue. Carcinoid syndrome, a form of cancer. Possibly immediate surgery.

I was not prepared for that and needed time to comprehend all that had taken place in such a short time. By now it was the wee hours of the morning, but I knew the people of our church were prepared to take special prayer requests at any hour, day or night. I asked my husband to call our pastor and get the prayer chain going and to call my sister, who attends another church, to start their prayer chain. My husband asked, "What exactly do you want them to pray for?" My reply was, "That I do not have to have surgery now and that God will take care of it." After a CT scan and other testing, a tumor was discovered on my appendix, and numerous other nodules appeared on the lungs. Had the cancer spread from the appendix? On Monday, the surgeon made the decision that I should stay in the hospital for observation for several days. If no further attacks occurred, I would be referred to a doctor in Virginia who specializes in this treatment. More doctors, more tests. I really don't have time for all this. This was the day we were to start a new Bible study: "Angels, Messengers of God." I was the instructor for a women's Bible study group and had already done much preparation. Determined that this group would start with or without me, I asked my pastor to make sure the study started that night. At 7 p.m. the phone rang in my hospital room, and the joyous voices of the ladies were calling to inform me they were all gathered and praying for me. Angels, Messengers of God, had started.

I was released the following day, with more appointments, other physicians to see, and more tests to go through. One of the tests consisted of an injection and testing in a machine that lasted approximately one hour. This testing would go on each day for five days. My husband and I traveled to Virginia, stayed in a hotel, and I kept my appointment at the hospital each day for the test, which consisted of being strapped on a bed, the bed sliding in and out of a machine as another machine rotated around my body. Intense and stressful as it was, I had asked the technicians if I could play an inspirational CD a friend, Chuck Conalogue, had recorded to sooth my soul and help the time pass peacefully. By Friday, the last day of testing, I knew the routine well. I literally climbed on the table (I am short). The technician strapped me in—ankles, thighs, hips, arms, chest—no movement was allowed, and the octreoscan began.

I had accepted Christ as my Lord and Savior many years ago, and He had walked with me through the good times and the bad times. I knew His presence was always there and that many prayers had been answered through the years. As I lay in that machine I did not pray for healing. I gave God all the praise and glory for all the good things that had happened in my life, many experiences too numerous to name.

Suddenly the machine started making a loud noise. All I could think of was the noise a garbage truck makes when it is backing up. The technicians came running in the room, removed the bed from the machine, and appeared to be searching for something. They were actually on their hands and knees on the floor looking and exploring with their hands. I was still strapped on the bed and asked them what was going on. They said an unexplained light had appeared on the monitor. They said possibly a previous technician accidentally dropped a needle on the floor, but there was no needle to be found. As they unfastened the straps around me, they searched the sheets to look for any foreign objects. I asked them if possibly there could be anything on my jacket hanging on the door that could trigger the machine. The comment was, "No, not unless your coat is radioactive. That's how strong the light was." Oh, I knew what that light was: the presence of the Holy Spirit was there, comforting me. But would these people with a medical background ever believe such a thing?

I was told, because of the appearance of the light and my removal from the machine, there was a good chance I may have to come back another day to complete the testing. My husband and I had already checked out of the hotel and were ready to travel three hours back home. I had seen enough of the hospital that week. As the technician strapped me in the bed again, I said to her, "I know you will think I am crazy and you may think I am lying, but 'that light' was the presence of the Holy Spirit in the room with me, comforting me.

She graciously said, "Oh, I do believe you."

I can tell you, I knew I had shaken her to a degree. She explained that the chances were slim to none that I would be in the same position as I was before the light appeared. As the technician strapped me in, I told her I did not feel like I was in the same position as before the interruption. At this point she was not going to argue with a crazy lady. After two other attempts, I told her I believed I was in the same position as before, and the test finally resumed. The two technicians stood quietly by the monitor in the room and watched as I slowly entered the machine. In all the chaos, I had forgotten about the music playing in the background. With everything very quiet and in anticipation of the right alignment of my body in comparison to before the disruption, I could hear the voice softly singing,

> *Oh I believe in miracles,*
> *one happens all the time,*
> *and when I least expect a miracle*
> *God will show something to ease my mind,*
> *like rainbows and sunshine.*

Had I experienced a miracle? Yes. The presence of God had manifested Himself through the light. But little did I know that was just the beginning. To the amazement of the technicians, I was in perfect alignment as before the light appeared, and the testing resumed. We returned home and I was anxious to share with my church, and anyone else who would listen, the good news about the light.

Several weeks passed with no word of the test results. While waiting, I realized nothing was being accomplished by staying at home, as my doctor had instructed me to do, so I returned to work in the gift shop my husband and I owned. That very day the physician phoned and informed me no cancer appeared. The needed surgery was completed. Several benign tumors were removed, along with my appendix, and other minor surgery to complete the process.

Today I am well and still praising God. Our ladies' Bible study group completed the "Angels, Messengers of God" study with a new outlook. Some tell me they believe an angel was with me in that room during the testing. I did not see the light; it appeared on the monitor that the technicians saw, but I certainly felt the presence of God. God's presence is always with us; He always stands beside us. Don't just call on Him in time of need. Fellowship with Him daily, and He will make His presence known to you. Endurance, character, hope—is God preparing you for something greater? I think so. May the peace of God be with you.

LOIS GRAY MILLER

BY GRACE WE ARE SAVED

In anticipation of Jesus' second coming,
I sat down to reminisce.
I wanted to contribute in some way
To the excitement and the bliss.
But instead God gave me this message,
To share with you the start
To look back on the moment,
When He came into my heart.

I was a lowly sinner
Unworthy of His grace.
But one night He reached down
And at last we met face to face.
There have been many heartaches and sorrows along the way,
But somehow Jesus makes it sweeter
Day by day!

I know not when He'll call me home,
Or where I'll be that day,
But let it be said,
"I followed Him all the way."

If for any reason
I have caused you to stumble or fall,
Just remember Calvary
And Jesus paid it all.

When I look at others,
And in them find some fault,
I try to think of Golgotha,
Where our sins were bought.
Oh, to be a great warrior
For His name I fought!
No, I am a mere sinner, whom He sought.
But what can be greater
Than to know that one day
I'll walk with my Savior,
"Dear Jesus come quickly!" I pray.

If you look at others,
And in them find some sin,
Won't you get on your knees and pray,
"Lord, cleanse them from within"?
For if we pray one for another
With compassion and great love,
Our Lord will surely answer,
And send peace like a dove.

LOIS GRAY MILLER

CLOSING TIME

So short a span our days on earth,
Then will the closing come.
So short a time to do our work
Before we hear that final drum.

Being about our Father's business
That's what we're set to do,
Before the final closing time
Making use of the days so few.

What have you done with your few years?
What will your answer be?
I truly hope that I can say,
"I have won souls for Thee."

My fondest hope when life is o'er
And the final race is run
Is to hear my Heavenly Father
Say to me, "Well done."

BARBARA M. AUSTIN

WITH GOD ALL THINGS ARE POSSIBLE

In 1990, after one of my brothers was diagnosed with colon cancer, I started having some of the same alarming symptoms. Several tests showed a large mass in my stomach. I was scheduled for a CT scan at the hospital in Norfolk. While waiting for this appointment, I had a visit from a former pastor and his wife, Glen and Mary Lawrence. Brother Glen asked if I was having any problems because the Lord had laid it on his heart to pray for me. He prayed, and we both had a great peace, the peace that passes understanding. I had the CT scan, and the results were a surprise to the doctor but not to me. He kept looking at the pictures and saying, "This is impossible." Holding up his fist, he said, "I saw that tumor, it was this big, and I knew it was cancer."

The doctor learned that day what Matthew 19:26 says: "With men this is impossible, but with God *all things* are possible." There had been a cancerous tumor, but God's power healed it.

Again in 2019 my body was attacked by cancer: stage 3 squamous cell carcinoma of the right lung. X-rays and CT scans showed the tumor was too large to be removed surgically. If you know the Lord at all, you know He is not moved by what tests say. Once again, Jesus Christ, my healer, came on the scene and removed the cancer without surgery. The last CT scan showed no cancer.

Again, Matthew 19:26: *"With men this is impossible, but with God all things are possible."*

Thanks be to God!

BARBARA MEEKINS AUSTIN

AFTER ALL THE WASTED YEARS

The devil only comes
to kill, steal, and destroy.

But through the One
I have gained access by faith
into His grace.

He has given me
Love, Peace, and Joy.

I let the devil for too long
drag me through the mud.

When I finally broke loose,
Christ was still there waiting
and washed me in His Blood.

So I write this to you
in suffering rejoice

Because, if you haven't heard
from me lately,
there is perseverance in my voice.
Perseverance builds character
and character Hope.

Now that's something you want,
want to drown out alcohol or dope.

So Salvation is Mine and
Vengeance is His

And for the rest of my life
in His will shall I live!

LIVED BY A KINNAKEETER,
WRITTEN BY CODY HARRIS

THE GLORIOUS EVENT

"Joy to the world; the Lord has come!"
We don't realize how glorious an event it was when Jesus came into the world as a baby. He was God! He grew up and walked among men. Think about it: Almighty God, creator of all things, all-powerful, walking and living among men. We are His creation. What compelled Him to do that? His great love for all mankind. He did not want to see all mankind destroyed again. He is not willing that anyone should perish. That glorious night, all heaven rejoiced!

"Let earth receive her king."
In the Bible, Luke 2:8–20 says that an angel of the Lord appeared to shepherds who were watching their sheep at night. It says the glory of the Lord shone around them. The angel said to them, "Do not be afraid, for behold, I bring you good tidings of great joy which will be to all people. For there is born to you this day in the city of David, a Savior, who is Christ the Lord.

"And suddenly there was with the angel a multitude of the heavenly host praising God and saying, 'Glory to God in the highest and on earth peace, goodwill toward men!'"

After the shepherds had hurried to see Jesus, they made widely known the saying that was told them concerning Him. The shepherds returned home glorifying and praising God, and they told a lot of people. When Joseph and Mary brought the young Jesus to the temple in Jerusalem to present Him to the Lord, a man there named Simeon said that the Holy Spirit had told him that he would not die until he had seen the Lord's Christ. Simeon took Jesus in his arms and blessed God. It was revealed to him that Jesus was the One that was to come. Simeon spoke blessings and prophesied over them. It says in Luke 2:25 that the Holy Spirit was upon Simeon. Can you imagine how wonderful it was for Simeon, after all those years, to finally see the Christ? A widow of great age was a prophetess who did not depart from the temple but served God with fasting and prayers night and day. The instant she saw Jesus, she also knew Jesus was the One. She gave thanks to the Lord and spoke about Him to everyone who was looking for redemption in Jerusalem. So there were some at that time who believed Jesus was their King.

"Let every heart prepare Him room."
Oh, that people would prepare their hearts and make room for Jesus. People's hearts can be so evil and deceitful by allowing things to come into their hearts and grow that there is no room for Christ. What if, from the beginning, after Jesus was born, all people followed Jesus? Can you imagine what the world would be like today? There would be peace on earth and goodwill toward all people! Oh, if everyone knew and understood the great love that God has for them. We need to let everyone know about the great love of God, so that they have a chance to prepare room in their hearts for Him.

"And Heaven and Nature sing."
Can you imagine how all heaven rejoiced on the night Jesus was born? It must have been one glorious celebration. The singing must have been beautiful. It says in Luke 19:40: "and He answered and said unto them, 'I tell you that if these should hold their peace, the stones would immediately cry out.'"

DARLENE SCARBOROUGH WILLIS

INDEPENDENCE DAY

My Savior died for you and me,
Upon that old rugged tree.
He carried our sins to the cross that day,
That we might have salvation and not have to pay.
The sins of man, though they are many,
Were paid for that day, to the last penny.
If you will bring your sins to Him and confess,
He will put on you a robe of righteousness.
He is our helper day by day,
If we just come to Him in love and pray.
Mankind is not perfect in any way,
So don't despair if you sin, just pray.
We need to open up His Word and read,
Because in the Bible, there is wisdom for all you need.
His Word still stands down through the ages,
All you have to do is open the Book and read its pages.
For your sins, our Savior did die.
So why not give Him your life? Just give Him a try.
You will not be disappointed or sad,
Because He will touch your life and make you glad.
You will be washed, cleansed, set free, and have a new start,
If only you will give Jesus your heart.

DARLENE SCARBOROUGH WILLIS

HEATHER'S STORY

Heather was a dear, close friend of my daughter, Diana. Now this was before Diana developed a close relationship with the Lord. She knew the Lord, but she wasn't where she is now. In her precommitment days, she and Heather would go out and drink together.

After Diana moved back from Texas because her dad had had quadruple bypass surgery, she had pretty much given up her wild ways. One night Heather asked Diana to go out drinking, but Diana told her she didn't do that anymore. "Diana, I've seen you when you should have been dead," Heather said. "There's been a protection over you that I don't have, but I would like what you've got."

Not walking in the fullness of the Lord's salvation, Diana couldn't share what she herself didn't yet have. All she said was, "You know my folks. They pray." That's all she got out. Heather did go out drinking that night. She became intoxicated. While she was driving home, she hit an abutment on Governor's Avenue by the old Assembly of God Church in Delaware.

At 4 a.m., Diana got the call.

"Do you know this woman? She was in an accident and is critically injured. We've taken her to Kent Hospital."

Diana immediately called me and asked to meet her at the hospital. Linwood (my husband) and I arrived before Heather's mother. Moments later, she arrived, went into her daughter's room, then returned distraught. The sight of her daughter bleeding was too much for her to handle.

I asked, "Would you mind if I went in to pray with your daughter?" She nodded her affirmation, so I entered Heather's room for what proved to be a life-changing moment for us both. Heather lay unconscious on the hospital bed. She was bleeding from her eyes, nose, mouth, and ears. Then the Lord spoke to me in my mind's eye. "I don't want you to pray for her," He said. "I want you to introduce me to her."

There was obviously no time to waste, so I spoke to this unconscious girl. "Heather, there's a man standing in front of you. His name is Jesus. He heard you when you said you wanted what Diana had. He heard the longing of your heart. All you have to do is accept the invitation and you'll have what your heart desires. He is reaching out His hand to you. Just take His hand and He'll walk you on over." I didn't feel a release in my spirit the first time, so I repeated the whole conversation again. And I said, "Heather, take His hand." Then I knew. Something in my spirit said that it was done. I knew. When I came out and sat down, I talked to Diana.

"You're not going to believe what happened." Then I told her what I just told you. She said, "I do believe."

Actually, that encounter with Heather was the fulfillment of a prophetic dream or vision the Lord gave me when Diana was about nine years old. I took Darvon one evening and discovered that I was allergic to it. As I was passing out, waves of darkness overwhelmed me. In that time I saw a carriage-drawn hearse coming toward me. Purple and scarlet flowers were overflowing. They covered the entire hearse.

Then a prophetic voice spoke to me, saying, "As close as you came to death, you're going to pull brands from the burning. They will be that close to the mouth of hell, and you'll reach down and grab them."

Heather died that night. Time passed. One morning I awoke from the strangest experience. I needed to speak to Diana, so I called her and asked her to have lunch with me. We went for lunch. As we spoke, I told her of the experience.

"I can't call it a dream or a vision," I said. "I'm not sure what it was, but I was in heaven. I heard the most beautiful music and sounds. I know the throne was there but I couldn't see it. I saw Heather kneeling and the angels all around. She was saying, 'Such mercy, such mercy, such mercy.' I came out of it knowing that Heather was in heaven."

Diana was crying. "Mom, you never mentioned her name since that day at the hospital. Never a day goes by that I haven't thought about Heather."

The Jewish people talk about the kaddish. One year after you die they have a celebration called the homecoming. They celebrate that their loved one is home. My experience occurred one year to the day, almost to the hour. It was dawn. She died somewhere around five or six.

God pulled back the heavens and let me have a glimpse into the celebration because my Jesus is Jewish. There was a celebration of Heather's homecoming. The Lord just pulled back the heavens and let me see part of it.

That experience changed my whole life. Before that I was judgmental. I thought that nobody could get drunk and go to heaven. Everything now that I see relates back to that. God is much more merciful than we are.

God sees the heart and the desires of the heart more than He sees behavior, but now I can relate to people based on that experience with Heather and the Lord.

Years later, I attended a prayer meeting. One of my cousin's sons ingested drugs and died during the night. Before he died, a day or so before, he was riding with his mom and he said, "Mom, I want to go home."

She said, "You are home."

"No, I want to go to heaven to be with Jesus."

A day or so later he died in his bed, having ingested drugs. I was in a regular prayer meeting on Tuesday night, and the Lord spoke to me. He told me to go down to North Carolina and share with his mom what happened with Heather. He said that his mom had lost hope.

So I went to North Carolina and shared with her what God had given me. She was comforted, and she now had hope that God is merciful.

You see, God also heard the cry of her child, who said, "I want to go home." We don't know what that cry was in his heart. Because the heart's cry was, "I want to go home," the Lord says, "come on up."

I'm not glorifying doing this, but I am saying that God's mercy is greater than our worst sin—that all we have to do is cry out to him. He forgives, and we're accepted and beloved even in a state of unconsciousness. Somewhere in our conscious state we have cried aloud and He heard and answered.

The scripture the Lord gave me was Acts 16:31: "Believe on the Lord Jesus Christ and thy shall be saved and thy household." So you have to answer this question: Do you believe the Bible or do you believe the circumstances?

PASTOR FAYE GRAY BALLANCE
DOVER, DELAWARE

FOUR THINGS GOD NEVER KNEW

The wages of sin is death—but the gift of God is eternal life through Jesus Christ our Lord.

ROMANS 6:23

God never knew of a sin that He did not hate
For sin is of Satan and will lead to man's fate.
Sin is like a cancer that will eat man's soul away.
So let us beware of the evil that is in our world today.

God never knew of a sinner that He did not love.
Sinners are God's children that He is always thinking of.
A sinner is a lost sheep that has wandered from the fold.
God will never cease to search him out and make him His very own.

God never knew a better plan of salvation than that He has
For He sent His son Jesus Christ to die on the cross for the good and the bad.
All of us are sinners saved by the grace of God.
Let us ever beware of that as on this earth we trod.

God never knew of a better time for us to be saved than now
For today is the day of salvation so let us make our vow
To serve Him all the rest of our days that we have on this land
And we will be sure to spend eternity upon that golden strand.

These are four things that God did not know
It is the very gospel truth for the Bible tells us so
And if by chance you never have given your life to Him
I beg of you to open up your heart and let Jesus Christ the Savior come and dwell within.

HERSCAL P. WILLIAMS

NO PRAYER IS EVER WASTED

My heart was heavy burdened
As I bowed there by my bed,
Recalling a lifetime of prayers
And countless tears I'd shed.

I cried out from my heart,
"Lord, where do my prayers go?
I know You hear them all,
For the Bible tells me so."

Then my eyes fell on the pages,
And your Word to me was shown.
Hope swelled within as I read,
"Your prayers are kept by my throne.

For no prayer is ever wasted;
I keep them in bowls made of gold.
They're the very fragrance of heaven;
Their aroma can never be told.

That precious pungent perfume
Is the essence that does pervade
The halls and streets of My city,
Gathered each time you pray."

My heart was filled with gladness
At that scene before the throne.
Our Father collects our prayers
To perfume His heavenly home!

To think that the sacred scent
Drifting on the heavenly breeze
Flows there from the faithful saints
Who spend time with Him on their knees.

All the prayers we pray
Fly straight to that heavenly realm.
They're the aroma in the nostrils of God
In the throne room of the Lamb!

JOYCE WILLIAMS

THE FRAGRANCE OF THE HOLY SPIRIT

Exodus 30:34–36. The Old Testament tells us how the Tabernacle was to be constructed and used. The altar of prayer, the golden incense-altar, stood just before the veil that concealed the Holy of Holies, where God's presence appeared. In addition, the instructions for worship were given along with the formula for incense. The ingredients were divinely prescribed.

In like manner, there were divine instructions concerning the elements that must mingle in acceptable prayer. It must be the prayer of faith. There must be penitence and contrition in it. It must contain thanksgiving and submission. It must be the kind of prayer that God has commanded, or it will not rise to heaven as sweet incense. What could be sweeter to God's senses than the sweet fragrance of our worship (prayers)?

2 Corinthians 2:14. During that era, upon returning home, a victorious general was honored with a parade. He would march with his army through the streets, displaying the spoils and the captives of war.

2 Corinthians 2:15–16. That procession included spices and incense, burning openly, which sent sweet aromas through the streets. The cheering crowds not only saw and heard the general's exploits, they smelled victory in the air. In the same way, we are witnesses to Christ's victory. Those who respond positively to the good news find life and mercy. But those who reject it face death and judgment.

There is an exquisite beauty in the thought that true prayer is a fragrance to God as it rises from the golden altars of believing, loving hearts. The pleadings and supplications of His people on earth are wafted up to him from lowly homes, from humble sanctuaries, from stately cathedrals, from sick rooms, and from the darkened chambers of sorrow when we realize our frailty—as the breath of flowers is wafted to us from rich gardens and fragrant fields.

In 1584 Philip Amadas and Arthur Barlowe arrived at the shores of what later became North Carolina. As they drew near the shore, the fragrance of flowers was in the air as if they were in some delicate garden. They sailed the coast and took possession of the country for the queen of England. Was that fragrance the fragrance of the Holy Spirit leading them to a land that would give the first settlers religious freedom?

Fragrant worship is only that which rises to God after it is poured on Christ. Christ is the truth through whom we must worship.

LOIS GRAY MILLER

ANGELS

RESCUED BY THE ANGELS

At the beginning of a Sunday night church service, our choir director announced that a young man from the island was missing and his girlfriend had called to request prayer for him. The young man, a Coast Guardsman stationed on a ship, had gone ashore with others while the ship was docked for repairs. He did not return to the ship and a search began for him. The pastor asked me to lead the congregation in special prayer for his safe return. As I prayed, in my mind I saw a young man falling off the dock, near the ship, and a legion of angels scooping down to retrieve the body. These multitude of celestial beings were so entwined that one faded into another. How could I verbalize what I had just seen? I kept the image to myself. During the service, the young man's girlfriend silently entered the church. At the end of the service, the pastor again asked the congregation to pray for her and her fiancé. I inquired more specifically about the details of his disappearance, but she had very little information. I already knew in my heart the outcome.

The next morning as my husband and I watched the early news on TV, an announcement came that divers were searching for the body of the young man. At that time I knew they would find the body because I had seen him the night before taken to heaven by the legion of angels. Eventually, I reluctantly shared my vision with a member of his family. I hoped this would in some way comfort them, knowing that although he was absent from them, he was present with the Lord. The image of this event will forever be etched in my memory.

I struggled with these images until the realization came to me that we have it on the authority of Jesus himself that God sends His angels for us as we end this earthly life. Luke 16:22 tells us about the beggar, Lazarus:

"And it came to pass, that the beggar died, and was carried by the angels into Abraham's bosom." That transition from this world to the next is made easier by these angelic beings. Angels themselves never die; they are immortal. They were created before the foundation of the earth was laid and will still be in existence for all eternity. Job 38:4–7 says, "When God laid the foundation of the earth, the morning stars sang together and all the angels shouted for joy." Angels were present at the creation of the earth.

But there is more to the story than just a heavenly escort. So why do the angels take us to heaven? Ephesians 6:12 says we wrestle against "spiritual hosts of wickedness in heavenly places." That is the theological explanation.

Simply put, there are three heavens: the first is the air we breathe or the atmospheric heaven: the blue skies where the birds fly. The technical term for this is the "troposphere" and above that is the "stratosphere." The second heaven, where the galaxy is located, is where the fallen angels have access: the spiritual realm where there is a constant battle between the angels of God and the angels of Satan. The third heaven is where God resides—you know, the pearly gates, the streets of gold and the mansions (with no mortgage payments), that heavenly abode where God is preparing a place for us and we will live forever. The third heaven where the presence of God dwells is secure.

So we have established the existence of three heavens. Have you made your reservation?

Back to the first and second heavens and the angelic escorts.

"In the beginning," God created Lucifer, the most beautiful, intelligent creature in God's creation and a member of the highest order of angels. Lucifer (Satan) aspired to a position of equality with God and fell because of pride over his personal beauty. Please remember that God created angels, including Satan, so Satan and God are not equal. God is the creator of all things! There are many names for Lucifer. Most people know him as Satan, and he is often referred to as the devil. Satan is also called Old Serpent, Great Dragon, Destroyer, Accuser, Deceiver, Angel of the Bottomless Pit, Apollyon, Belial, Beelzebub, God of This World, Murderer, Prince of This World, Ruler of Darkness, Antichrist, Tempter, Unclean Spirit, and Wicked One. Does this give you some idea of his personality?

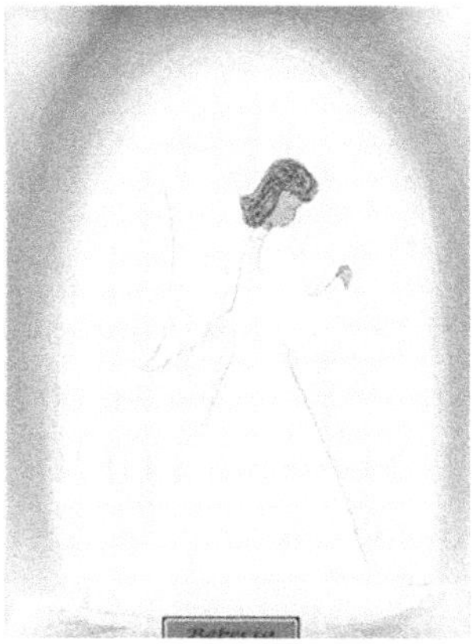

Psalm 91:11: "For He shall give His angels charge over you to keep you in all your ways."
ARTWORK BY LOIS G. MILLER

Lucifer, created perfect in all his ways, became rebellious. He was cast out of heaven along with one-third of the angels that joined his rebellion. He came down to earth, where he became the prince of the power of the air, igniting the conflict of the ages between God and Satan and thus necessitating angels escorting the dead to heaven.

Angels know their enemies (fallen angels) and their strategy. Angels know what the enemy has done in the past. God wants us to be informed about our adversaries.

We know the outcome of our spiritual warfare. Satan will be defeated, and believers in Jesus Christ will reign triumphantly with Him forever. In the meantime, know that when it is time for that glorious trip to heaven, you will have a royal escort to the pearly gates with great rejoicing!

LOIS GRAY MILLER

CORONAVIRUS

Near the conclusion of writing this book, I had no idea that a pandemic would viciously engulf our world. The coronavirus, an infectious disease also known as COVID-19, does not just attack the immune system. This deadly disease has also infected the foundation of our free society. It has upended life as we know it in countless ways. One particularly difficult change is its impact on the way we mourn the loss of loved ones.

On April 5, 2020, my sister, Rebecca Gray, suffered congestive heart failure and out of the reach of many family members went to be with her heavenly Father. She was known for her strong faith in God and her gentle, loving spirit. My sister truly believed there is an afterlife and that she would be wonderfully received in the arms of a loving God. She did not fear death.

During this pandemic, we had to modify the way we said good-bye. When she died, family members who would have traveled from other places could not be at her bedside holding her hand.

Traditional funeral rites and family gatherings could not be performed. On top of everything else, the coronavirus stole our ability to properly grieve. Not having access to people stepping in and taking care of one another is devastating. There is a closure that comes with funerals, with burials, with being able to physically be there and say good-bye in person. In Kinnakeet, death has always meant a time of coming together for our small, close-knit community where everyone is family or a neighbor.

The Bible has a unique view of death for those who have placed their trust in Jesus Christ, as my sister had done. The Bible describes death for the believers as "falling asleep." "But I do not want you to be ignorant, brethren, concerning those who have fallen asleep, lest you sorrow as others who have no hope" (1Thessalonians 4:13). The Bible also describes death for the believer as "absent from the body and to be present with the Lord" (2 Corinthians 5:8). As my sister made this pilgrim flight from this world to the next, we are assured that angels escorted her to that heavenly abode where God resides and where He is preparing a place for us. Luke 16:22 tells us of the story of Lazarus": "And it came to pass that the beggar died, and was carried by the angels into Abraham's bosom." Luke 24:51 tells us that when Jesus died, "He was carried up into Heaven" by angels.

Yes, my sister was carried to heaven by angels but she did not become an angel. We do not become angels when we die and go to heaven. It has become popular in our culture to say, "Heaven gained another angel," when someone dies. I realize this is probably an expression we use but we need to be aware that angels are spiritual beings that God created to be His servants, and God has given them great authority and power to do His will. Humans are one kind of God's creation, and angels are another. To say we become angels is to say we stop being humans.

Angels are spirit beings created by God and were created simultaneously—in a single moment. When did God create angels? Angels were on the scene to celebrate when the earth was created. When God laid the foundation of the earth, "the morning stars sang together and all the angels shouted for joy" (see Job 38:4–7).

Angels are messengers of God. Unlike us, they never grow old, never get sick, never go to the hospital, never marry, and never die. Thus they are free to give their full devotion to God.

What a comfort to know when we leave this earth, we do not go alone into the presence of God. Angels are the escorts that will carry us with shouting and great joy.

Hallelujah!

LOIS GRAY MILLER

LIVELIHOOD

US LIFE SAVING STATIONS OF THE OUTER BANKS

No discussion about the history of Kinnakeet (Avon) would mean anything without first realizing how the area was so closely tied to saving mariners' lives. The sea has played an important role in transportation and commerce throughout our nation's history. An unfortunate consequence of the nation's dependence on water transportation in the 18th and 19th centuries was the death of sailors and passengers due to shipwrecks.

After the wrecks of the *Metropolis* and the *Huron* in 1877, it was decided that life-saving stations along the Outer Banks of North Carolina would be placed no fewer than three miles apart and no more than seven miles apart. This was a crucial decision for the stations to be effective. The original seven stations built in 1874 were spaced 12 to 15 miles apart, leaving critical gaps along the beaches that could not be monitored.

Little Kinnakeet Life Saving Station

Little Kinnakeet was one of the first seven life-saving stations erected on the Outer Banks. Little Kinnakeet Life Saving Station was established north of what is today known as Avon. These were all 1874-type designs, and all built in 1874. A kitchen/mess room was added to Little Kinnakeet in 1892. In 1900 the original station was moved to the west side of the highway. It was converted to a boathouse in 1904 when a southern-pattern station house was added to the southeast corner of the grounds. The station was deactivated June 14, 1954.

Big Kinnakeet Life Saving Station

Big Kinnakeet Life Saving Station was located south of Avon near Askins Creek. Big Kinnakeet was especially important because it had a lifeboat station on its grounds. Smaller than a life-saving station, a life-boat station stood around 24 feet from top to bottom and included a loft. It stored additional boats and equipment. Placed near the water, life-boat stations included a ramp for easy access to the sand. Big Kinnakeet Life Saving Station was severely damaged by a hurricane in 1944, and was later leveled and never rebuilt.

So what was life like along the desolate shores of the Outer Banks? What did it take to be a surfman in the Life Saving Service? The best surfmen were often fishermen who knew the waters well around the inlets, bays, and turbulent sea. They had the experience and stamina needed to swing the heavy oars of the surfboats. Even when the gasoline motor had been developed, rowing out past the shoals was still necessary before they could be started.

Daily life was often numbingly routine. Drills ranged from launching the surfboat, beach apparatus (breeches buoy) drill, and first aid training, with a certain day of the week dedicated for each. When drills were not taking place, surfmen were assigned tower watches or beach patrols. Time was also reserved for painting and the upkeep of the station. The station's keeper was tasked with overall supervision of the station and surfmen. Rescues could be needed at any time during all kinds of weather.

Idle time was spent with families, reading books and magazines, fishing, and farming. Sundays were dedicated to worship. Eventually villages sprang up around the stations with hubs of activity.

The stations had somewhat of a warm, familylike atmosphere toward islanders traveling and stopping in. The stations were famous for their abundant meals and willingness to feed islanders who were stuck in the sand or trapped in a storm.

On January 28, 1915, President Woodrow Wilson signed the Act to Create the Coast Guard, merging the Life Saving Service with the Revenue Cutter Service to create the United States Coast Guard.

Dallas R. Miller retired from the Coast Guard at the Little Kinnakeet Life Saving Station, three miles north of Avon, on March 1, 1985. The retirement ceremony included crew members from Group Cape Hatteras dressed in uniforms from the era of the Life Saving Service.

Senior Chief Miller chose the Little Kinnakeet Life Saving Station as the location for his retirement ceremony because his grandfather, William Bembry Miller, retired there in May 1936 after 32 years of service in the Life Saving Service and Coast Guard, all at this station. Also, Senior Chief Miller's father, Dallas B. Miller, retired in January 1944 at Little Kinnakeet Station after 12 years of service at various locations within the Coast Guard, including Little Kinnakeet Station.

John B. Miller (brother; bottom center), Dallas R. Miller (back left), Dallas B. Miller (back center), John B. Miller Jr. (back far right)

There is a long history of Coast Guard careers in the Miller family. Senior Chief Miller's grandfather had five sons who enlisted in the Coast Guard. In the next generation, seven of the sons made the Coast Guard their career. These 13 men have provided at least 250 years of cumulative service in the Coast Guard. Most families of the island can recount an impressive genealogy of ancestors and relatives who served in this capacity.

AVON (KINNAKEET) HARBOR

Photo taken from a United States Coast Guard aircraft the day the dredging of the Kinnakeet Harbor was completed in 1946. The lower part of the photo shows the wing of the plane. Before the dredging, boats were anchored along the Pamlico Sound shoreline.

PHOTO COURTESY OF WAYNE GRAY

All the water in the world,
however hard it tried,
could never, never sink a ship
unless it got inside.

All the hardships of this world
might wear you pretty thin,
but they won't hurt you, one least bit,
unless you let them in.

UNKNOWN AUTHOR

AVON HARBOR, 1977
The late afternoon sun casts its last glimmer of light onto a boat and dock that snuggle up to the harbor of Avon, overlooking the Pamlico Sound. In foreground is Avon Worship Center.

THEN AND NOW—AVON HARBOR
LEFT: *"Ernie" (dog) enjoying a swim at the south end of the harbor. Photo circa 1973*

RIGHT: *Docks are gone at the south end of the harbor, and the north end of harbor is slowly filling in with sand. Photo January 2020*

(From left) Dallas Miller, Manson Meekins, Herschal Williams, Bobby Gray, Carol Etheridge (Division of Marine Fisheries), Maxton Scarborough, and Earl O'Neal

THE *MYRT*

ARTWORK BY LOIS G MILLER

'Twas the night before a long haul
Still dark from the sun's fall,
my dad and I waiting for the alarm clock to call
Anticipation so great that it almost hurt,
knowing we would be soon underway in the Myrt.

Now the Myrt was an old boat, a workhorse for sure.
She's seen slick "cam" days,
and cut through the biggest of the Pamlico sound waves.
Every day of the week she pulled a twenty-two-hundred-yard net,
her engine would purr as to not even break a sweat.

Now, as with all things, she got older and her keel started to bend—
her hull started to rot and the broken ribs we could not mend.
So we took her to the "old mill creek," her days of fishing had come to an end and that really hurt,
But my dad and I shared something very special;
we got to sail together on a boat called the Myrt.

JOHN MILLER JR., MAY 2011

FISHING IN THOSE DAYS AND TIMES

(Robert) Watson Gray's Life and Experience on Hatteras Island, 1908–1989

"About 1934 we were fishing out of Hatteras Inlet, and in those days and times, there were so many boats around three o'clock in the morning when we'd leave, it would look like a little city going out towards the Diamond Shoals."

Watson Gray, who has been fishing almost all of his 72 years and has fished almost every different way—drop netting, long netting, crabbing, oystering—paused, then continued talking about his experiences drop net fishing for bluefish with Edward Scarborough, another Kinnakeeter (Watson's wife Isabella was Edward's sister).

Robert Watson Gray

"Went out there one day and there were big seas rolling on the Outer Diamonds and one hit us sideways and threw me overboard. There were cork jackets on the cabin, and I'd just told Edward that he'd better tie his boots down in case something should happen. I went way under and when I was coming up to the top, Edward's boots were going down by me, and when I got up to the top there were two cork jackets, one on each side of me, it was a good thing because I was out of breath, and I just reached over and put one on, and Edward asked me, 'What's the trouble with you? You sound like you're out of breath.' I said, 'If you'd been as far down under that water as I've been, you'd been out of breath too!'

"We had to go in the cabin and chink [repair a crack] two places in the boat where the sea had busted it, when the boat fell off the top of it. There were about four seas that went together and threw us in the air and she came down and hit it so hard that it burst the bottom of the boat. We had one big tool box and it shifted from one side of the boat to the other. We came on ashore, but that didn't stop us from fishing. We kept it right on up until the season was over, and the next year we moved up to New Inlet [north of Rodanthe], which hadn't been long cut through.

"We tried it up there for a season, there and Oregon Inlet, and times were pretty hard in those days and times, you know. We'd go out during the day and probably get in about dark and sometimes we'd have to carry fish as far as Wanchese, but most of the time we carried them to Rodanthe. I've seen it so hard in those days and times, when we were fishing, I'd catch fish here in Avon and run them to Hatteras and only get one half cent a pound for croakers. Brother, if you had to live like that in these days and times you'd be in a mess.

"New Inlet was 20 feet deep in some places and four feet on the bar, but from there on out there was deep water all the way out to the back of the reef. We'd fish during the day and then nights we'd run our nets out in the sound and catch bluefish and sell them, then we'd go back out in the ocean that day fishing.

"We fished together about three seasons like that in the ocean. And we didn't only fish for bluefish, we drop netted for grey trout and croakers in the winter. We only caught the blues in the spring of the year, from March on up until we quit fishing in June. We stood up on top of the cabin to look for the schools of the bluefish. When they were coming near us, sometimes they wouldn't come to the top. They'd come right close to the top and we could see a dark bed of them. That is when we would set our net, but sometimes the gulls would hit them. I remember an old wreck on the west side of the Outer Diamond. One fellow set around the wreck, thought it was a school of bluefish and tore his net up trying to get the net off.

"You'd just go out there and when you'd see a school of fish you'd take your boat and make a circle and take them in. I know one time Edward and I were coming in Hatteras Inlet.

"Mr. Erv Stowe, Edward's father-in-law, was ahead of us, and both crews had been out fishing all day and we hadn't caught a thing. About half a mile inside the inlet, Erv Stowe put a flag in the air for us to come to him, he'd made a set onto a big school of fish. I think he got about 3,000 or 4,000 pounds and we got about 2,000 pounds by backing him up. Here we'd been fishing out in the ocean all day and had to come clean inside the inlet to make our day's wages.

"We'd leave between three and four o'clock in the morning and tried to be to the Outer Diamond by daylight. We cooked aboard the boat. We had a cookstove, and sometimes we'd sleep aboard the boat, but sometimes we stayed at Erv Stowe's, room and boarding there with them.

"That was back in the days of dirt roads, and we couldn't go back and forth because it would take too long. We'd just stay down there, we'd come ashore and spend the night and then go out the next day. We'd come home every weekend until fishing was over. Mrs. Jennette B. Stowe, Edward's mother-in-law, tied most of our net. It would keep me and Edward busy filling two needles for her to tie them, she could tie them that fast. Most of our nets back in those days were hand tied. Mrs. Jennette tied us about four hundred yards, and we had some net we were using off a long net."

Mr. Gray said that they had to lime or wash the older netting every day, but you can fish the new nets for a week or two and just throw them in a tub with Clorox and they are as clean as the day you bought them. They bought their leads (sinkers) for 20 cents a pound, compared to a dollar a pound today, and they used real corks for floats. The nets they used to catch croakers and grey trout were 80 meshes deep and two-and-three-quarters-inch stretch mesh. The nets for catching bluefish were 45 to 50 meshes deep and four-inch stretch mesh. They used quarter-inch cotton lines in those days.

"No one else from Avon was fishing out on the ocean. The fishermen were from Wanchese, Manteo, and there were a lot of Core Sounders [eastern Carteret County] fishing there at the time. It would look like a little city going out in the morning. Everyone had their running lights on."

At that time, Watson and Edward were using a boat that Rocky Rollinson built. It had a six-cylinder Chevy engine and drew about 20 inches. "It was 36 feet long, deadrise, smart as a steel trap. A long, slim boat. I know one time it was rough and we kept swinging around the inlet, didn't know what to do about getting in. We saw a small sea and we caught it and ran it clean on in the inlet without catching another sea. We just kept it right behind us. We had to get across the bar and it was rough and we just struck a smooth time and came on in on one sea. Only luck!

"Gas was 20 cents a gallon, and you got a rebate of five cents, so it really cost you 15 cents a gallon. We were all mechanics in those days and times. We didn't have to carry our work somewhere. We did it ourselves. It didn't cost us much.

"You had to be a millionaire to own a marine engine. We fishermen hardly knew what a marine engine was. When we were set netting, we used what is called a 'make-and-break' engine. In those days, there was plenty of old junk laying around that you could pick up and put on the engines for parts. You had to crank them yourself. They would make about five miles per hour, and that was wide open. Now that was for set netting in the sound. In the ocean we used six-cylinder or even eight-cylinder engines, whatever you could get cheap, you know.

"It was really hard times in those days. We got half a cent a pound for croakers. I've carried croakers I caught long netting from Avon to Hatteras for half a cent a pound. That was 50 cents a box. They were large croakers. They called them drum croakers down there. Frazier Peele told me that if I hadn't sold him those fish he would have been ruined on some small ones he had bought off another fellow. Fifty cents went a long way in those days and times. Now you can't even have a drink and a piece of cake for

50 cents. Fifty cents is gone right there, but at one time you could take 50 cents and feed a family on it for a day. If a man had a hundred dollars in those days and times he was called 'Mister'!"

During the era of the Depression, Watson Gray said that he thought that people made out better on the island than anywhere else because of their access to free fish, clams, oysters, and crabs, and because they had gardens and chickens. The islanders mainly just had to buy a little bread. "I'm 72 years old and I'm still living, so after all we didn't starve to death. I mean we couldn't get the meats down here in those times. We had seafood, vegetables. Most of the stuff we had came out of a can, like canned beef, and beef in barrels. Half-a-ham and ham hocks were put up in pork barrels. I'd say these were 50-pound barrels. That's the way my mother and father [Mary and Obbie Gray] used to buy it. You didn't go out and buy a five-pound bag because I don't imagine a bag of flour would last over three or four days in our house. We had a big family. There were about ten of us including the parents."

When Watson Gray was 20, he went to New Jersey to work awhile, then joined the Coast Guard. In 1931, he came back to Avon and made a long net rig and started long netting and drop netting. Then he worked at the naval shipyard in Norfolk, Virginia, until he retired. When he came back he made another long net and started long netting, set netting, and drop netting. "I've had two or three little pound nets," he said, "and about eight or nine long nets in my life, and they've halfway wore me out, instead of me wearing them out."

Of all the ways of fishing, he says he prefers long netting. "It's the hardest, but I'd rather do it. It's more exciting. You bunt [the bagging part of a net] up some times, catch a dozen speckled trout or so, and think you're going to get rich but when you bunt you might sometimes just get an oyster shell or conch. Then sometimes you won't catch a one and you'll bunt up and have three, four, five thousand pounds. It's hard to tell. But the speckled trout are not here like they used to be. It used to be from the middle of August on up to around March or April you could figure on around one, two, three or up to five thousand pounds every set you made. That's when we fished on the back of the reef, but in the channel we could catch croakers and spots and scrap fish.

"I believe we caught more fish in those days and times than we do now because to start with we only used 900 to 1,100 yards of net and we would catch two or three boatloads, and we'd stake them off and bail out all the next day we'd catch so many. Now we use around 2,200 yards and sometimes we make ordinary catches and sometimes good catches. Way back then it was nothing to take a 200-yard swipe net along the shore. People used to make a living off of that, just catching them at night.

"Yet I've also seen it so hard that we'd come in from long netting of a day and catch nothing. Willis, Jarvis, and I would go north and break out our mullet nets and mullet net all night long. Of course these days and times I don't know if the fellows do that or not. I don't do it too many nights, but it would happen that way though. You had to live, you know.

"I've done about all kinds of fishing, drop netting, long netting, pound netting, set netting, mulleting. Tried all kinds. I've also done oystering, clamming, and crabbing. On the island in the '30s my brother Cyril, brother-in-law Burgess, and I went to Oregon Inlet and New Inlet and caught clams and sold them for 50 cents for 100 to Chauncy Meekins and Alvin Williams, and they would take them off the island and sell them. And then oystering, I've done a lot of oystering. We also sold them for around 50 cents a bushel. That was what they used to call the good ol' days, but I didn't see too much good about them the way you had to work for a living.

"I've also crabbed a lot. When I first started crabbing with Edward we crabbed down at Hatteras and we used trotlines. About a thousand yards of line and we used tripe [bait] on it. I know one time we were down there fishing and a fellow went out crabbing that day and he put his tripe on his line and went to the other end and waited for the crabs to get baited up good. And when he ran down his line to get crabs, the crabs had eaten all his tripe off his lines, and he had to come to shore to rebait.

"We would fix our lines at night. We had a big barrel and we'd stir it up and drop our fish line down in the barrel to keep the tripe so it would be in good shape for the next day, and some of us would use eel, but eel cost so much you couldn't hardly get that. We rigged a dipper over our sides and we had a roller over it so that, when the crab came to the roller, it would hit the roller and fall down into our scoop, and when that got pretty near full we'd have to stop the boat and lift the dipper up, and throw them in barrels. Sometimes we'd catch as high as five barrels a day. We sold them by the barrel in those days. We didn't sell them by the pound. That was three and four hours' work. We probably got three dollars or four dollars a barrel for them, about three cents or four cents a pound. At the price of stuff in those days and times, we really got more for crabs than we do today. The pots now will cost you ten dollars apiece rigged up and that line you'd buy would run you about three dollars or four dollars. Our bait would run us a couple dollars a day, something like that." Watson Gray said that local commercial fishermen did not start using wire crab pots until 1940 or 1945. Then a pot properly rigged up only cost a $1.50 to $2 apiece.

Watson Gray slowly paddling his boat across Avon Harbor, 1975

Now 72 years old and still living in Avon, Robert Watson Gray has done just about all kinds of fishing. He has owned eight or nine long rigs and many boats. When Mr. Gray was not working at the naval shipyard in

Virginia, where he worked for 15 years, and when he was not in the Coast Guard, he was probably spending his time fishing, as he is doing to this day.

INTERVIEW BY BRYAN GRAY
SEA CHEST, SPRING–SUMMER 1980

HUNTING

History of Hunting on the Outer Banks

Long before the surfers, kite boarders, and windsurfers discovered the beauty and exceptional sporting conditions of the Outer Banks, hunters were frequent visitors. Historically, the most popular form of hunting was, of course, waterfowl hunting. With duck hunting season from October through March, depending on the type of duck you plan to hunt, it brings back many memories of a bygone era.

Currituck, an Indian name for "Land of the Wild Goose," first became known as the duck hunting capital of the East Coast in the late 1800s. Adventurous sportsmen from the North began coming to the Outer Banks for the hunting, and in 1857, a group of northern sportsmen led by New York City attorney Philo T. Ruggles bought 3,100 acres for a dollar an acre and incorporated the Currituck Shooting Club. The club was the second hunting club incorporated in the United States and the first in North Carolina. In the late 1800s and early 1900s, visitors first arrived on Hatteras Island in the form of wealthy hunters and fishermen. Hunt clubs were established (and are now long gone). The largest on Hatteras Island was the 1,500-acre Gooseville Hunt Club in Hatteras Village. Many other hunt clubs were strewn throughout the Outer Banks. A lot of hunting activity in Avon centered on the Phipps Lodges. Not only was hunting a great sport, but the waterfowl was sold and transported to New York, where the game birds were distributed to restaurants in the city.

John Devine Farrow and Wilson "Wilse" Farrow, brothers from Avon, carved decoys and took out hunting parties for Cyrus Hooper, a Coast

Guardsman responsible for taking dignitaries hunting. John and Wilse were in charge of the blinds, decoys, and guiding.

There are many memories to share of the good ol' days with family stories about hunting, feather beds, and stewed goose. Ah, memories. What about you? Ever sleep on a feather bed or with a feathered pillow or had stewed goose for dinner?

The beds were valuable possessions, and people even made wills promising them to the next generation. Feathers for a feather bed would be saved from waterfowl being prepared for cooking. John Denver even wrote a song titled "Grandma's Feather Bed." As a young child growing up we had goose feather pillows and a feather bed that was handmade with the classic striped ticking. Ticking is the general term for a heavy cotton fabric used to cover feather beds or pillows. Many people consider baked pheasant (sometimes referred to as pheasant under glass) a delicacy, but a true Kinnakeeter would choose stewed goose any day. Stewed goose is prepared just like stewed chicken (chicken and dumplings), but substituting goose or duck for chicken.

LOIS GRAY MILLER

MR. RICHARD'S GEESE

A group of tame geese, long ago
Lived in Mr. Richard Hooper's backyard pound;
They ate and waddled to and fro
Contented though earthbound.

They wandered about aimlessly,
When the hunters they were not pleasing,
By luring their kin out on the reef
Up for a shot during hunting season.

Sometimes in November when wild geese soar
They'd flap their useless wings and try
To rise from earth as in days of yore
And over the Banks to fly.

But soon it seemed their striving ceased
And days were spent in useless living;
Indulging appetite and at ease
Waddling about with no misgiving.

Once Mr. Wall and friends were using
The geese for decoys out on the reef;
One mistook the decoys for wild geese
And shot them, ending the poor geese's grief.

Lord, forbid that I should grow too fond
Of earth and too much at ease
That I'd miss your call and not respond
And on to greater heights to rise.

BROOKSIE MEEKINS KUHL

Wilse Farrow and John Walter Barnes

THE HUNTERS

Once Uncle John and Wilse's hunting went well;
They brought in their fowl to the Mill Creek to sell.
Two customers came early and stood waiting by
When one fat goose took both ladies' eye.

One snatched the fowl yelling, "I want this goose!"
With the other lady pulling the head it came loose.
The situation was out of the hunter's control.
They stood openmouthed when the goose's head rolled.

Viewing the mangled goose, one lady relented.
Each chose another fowl, but neither repented
For the goose's destruction; they paid a pittance
And took off for home. Wilse exclaimed, "Good riddance!"

BROOKSIE MEEKINS KUHL

D. F. MEEKINS GENERAL STORE

The store opened in nineteen twenty-one
Newly painted floors fairly shone;
Shelves filled on walls along both sides;
Glass display cases full on counters wide.

Yard goods to be measured from the bolt,
Readymade cloths also to be sold;
Penny candy in the case to the right
With many colored gems, children's delight.

Sou'westerns, boots, and netting hung,
Line and net needles for fishermen;
Gunshells for hunters on the birdin' ground,
Lumber and nails for the carpenter, sold by the pound.

There were barrels of beef, corned beef and "No'thern,"
No'thern beef pickled in brine was the one most desired;
There were wheels of cheese, and coffee grinder,
A grinder for pepper there you would hand wind.

Upon the northeast wall were boxes of shoes—
There were Polly Parrot and the Star Brand;
We children loved to try on the new ones
Especially the high-heeled ones looked so grand.

Up the center aisle were fishhooks, corks, and netting
And things the gardener would need to own;
Guns the hunter would be needing
For hunting geese, in and out of season.

Yards of blue and white ticking were sold
For covers for pillows and for feather bed
To guard against the bitter Arctic cold
Of our bedrooms when blew the wintry winds.

The southeast corner held many a medicine;
One for anything that ailed you;
Quinine for malaria, peppermint for indigestion,
The dreaded castor oil for colds and flu.

A bin was filled with feed for the chickens—
Another held oats for the horse's feed.
Mr. Tom Meekins made a regular visit.
For this for Baking Powder his faithful steed.

Mr. Tom and horse and cart came about noontime.
We children often hailed him for a ride
On our way home from school at lunchtime;
He let us pile in; eight could get inside.

There we sat, Ena and Erskin Hooper,
Merian Meekins, Wilma and Hilda Gray,
Ena Meekins and Lucy O'Neal—all No'therners;
Sad to say but only four of us are around today.

Mr. Tom was oblivious to the crowd around him
Conversed with Baking Powder all the way;
Tied him to the post and then he went in
For his feed and to visit a good part of the day.

Alonzo Gray and John Devine Farrow,
His brother Wilse and John Walter Barnes,
Came to pass the time—all Little Kinnakeeters
Who abandoned their village and moved to Avon.

The woodstove stood at the store's center.
These were the years before electricity came.
Friends visited often in the cold of winter
And friendships were forged never to change.

Midwives tended folk at birth and the dying,
And when storms came and took their homes
Little Kinnakeeters helped each other in surviving;
Self-sufficient, but not alone.

The storekeeper was church superintendent.
At Christmas great cans of candy he'd need.
Boxes were packed for each child in attendance
And put 'neath the tree at church Christmas Eve.

A little boy once the store visited
Asked if he went to church, he said that he
Had no Sunday suit for church attending;
He was promised a suit if he went regularly.

He was given the suit and he did as he promised
Went to Sunday school and full member became;
That was just one of the many deeds of kindness
That D. F Meekins did at his general store.

The Mighty Midgetts of life-saving fame,
John Allen, Rasmus, and Levene came;
Folks traveled north from as far away as
Buxton, Trent, and even Hatteras.

Dorcas Ellen worked there for many a year
Serving customers always with good cheer;
Sometimes in a fit of giggles, she being shy
When Dr. Gatling his daily apple would buy.

His description he'd begin some distance away
Of the apple he wanted to purchase that day;
"Juicy, delectable, delicious and sweet."
The adjectives varied from week to week.

When wintry winds blew about the store
Charles built a woodfire in the stove;
Much is and lore was told of life in early days
Of shipwrecks and lifesavers and their ways.
Of Ben Daily and his rescue stories were told
How near Christmastime in 'ninety-four
A blizzard blew and made a battering sea
And a distress flag was raised off Kinnakeet.
"I'm going," called Captain Dailey. "Who goes with me?"
Creed's Hill surfmen with the crew would be.

All Big Kinnakeet surfmen would go along
As into the stormy sea the surfboat was launched.

Ben Dailey and the crew fairly fought their way
Through a dense fog and a perilous sea;
Toward the Ephraim Williams whose nine seamen frantic,
Fought Death in the Graveyard of the Atlantic.

Clutching floating timbers the seamen's cries
Were heard through the mist as the day died;
The surfmen drew them in from the ocean's maul
Nine men distraught at Death's close call.

They headed west toward Kinnakeet shore,
Each hour it seemed louder, the tempest roared;
Finally reached the shore through a sea "impassable,"
God and Ben Dailey doing the impossible.

Fields, the storekeeper, told of early days
Sailing in his schooner before his sight failed;
No bitterness had he, no time for tears
Neither was there complaining nor spoken fears.

He held always fast to God's promises
And in the darkness never failed to witness;
The storekeeper and his friends are gone away
But in memory will live always.

BROOKSIE MEEKINS KUHL

THE RUTH

Edward Scarborough worked with my father on his schooner *The Ruth*. When they docked at Elizabeth City or Norfolk my father would give Edward the orders for the merchandise he wanted to buy and with it a check for what the merchandise would cost. He was taking it for granted that the price would be the same as it had been the time before when he had bought it. He would say, "If this amount isn't right, tear up the check." It would always turn out to be the right amount. This he did, because he could not bear to owe anyone anything; if he did, it had to be paid before night fell. My father would not ever have had a credit card; his bill was paid the minute it was incurred.

Mr. Field's Schooner The Ruth
PAINTING BY BROOKSIE MEEKINS KUHL

When my father died in 1963, the world as Bankers had known it was disappearing. Honest thrift was becoming openly denounced; economy was becoming an old-fogy idea. People began spending their way into prosperity, with "Let the government keep you!" becoming their motto. These ideas were foreign to the old-timers of the Banks.

Edward was a very quiet, easygoing person, and he was my father's right-hand man. After my father lost his eyesight in the mid-forties, he depended more and more upon Edward to keep the boat in shape and the business going. I think my father loved him like one of his sons. They were both devout Christians and talked to one another about their faith. Edward had been in the freighting business since leaving the Coast

Guard. When he was a young man he worked with his grandfather Farrow Langford Scarborough on his boat carrying freight. In the late forties my father sold Edward *The Ruth,* and he used the boat for freighting until the storm of 1944 wrecked it.

SEAWEED: CASH CROP FROM THE SOUND

Edward Scarborough of Avon started baling seaweed when he was around 12 or 14 years old. He worked for his grandfather F. L. Scarborough, who was gathering and baling seaweed full-time.

"I remember my grandfather had probably 8 to 10 people working at the time," said Mr. Scarborough, "and there were several of we boys who would work with him. I think we got about 50 cents per day, which was a lot of money at that time." They baled seaweed on the soundside, where Mr. F. L. Scarborough owned a tract of land. They had a large building that was used for storage after the seaweed was baled, together with equipment that included boats and small barges, called flats. To bale the seaweed, they used pitchforks to spread it upon the shoreside, where it had to be turned once or twice until dry. To get a sufficient amount of seaweed, a tract of land between Big Kinnakeet and Little Kinnakeet was worked. The tract was owned at the time by Mr. Edward Scarborough's great-uncle, also named Edward Scarborough. When the seaweed was dry, it was baled by equipment similar to that used to bale hay.

"My grandfather used to build his own, which was called a seaweed baler," said Mr. Scarborough. "He would have all the hardware, which included what we call hooks, levers, and strong backs and so forth, made up at an iron foundry in Elizabeth City, North Carolina, and he would build the rest of it from there, which included press doors and so forth. It was all hand operated by using what we called a press, which was made of wood and pressed down by what we called a strong back operated by hooks and levers. It was packed in 100-pound bales and held together with wire, which we called 'baling wire,' and looked like, and was about the size of, a bale of hay."

The baled seaweed was sold to the Wren David Mattress Company in Virginia.

"My grandfather owned a two-masted sailboat at that time named the *Julia Bell*, which was used to haul freight from Elizabeth City and Avon," said Mr. Scarborough. "It was 54 feet long and 14 feet beam, and would haul 25 tons of merchandise. The seaweed was hauled to Elizabeth City by boat and loaded aboard railroad freight cars there and went the rest of the way by rail.

THE LUCINDA DOLL
In honor of Lucinda J. Gray (September 11, 1855–October 17, 1950)

Around the turn of the century, Ms. Lucinda would occupy some of her time by designing dolls. She would gather seaweed from the shoreline and use it to stuff the dolls for her grandchildren.

"The mattress company used the seaweed as an inside filler with an outside layer of cotton, I believe," added Mr. Scarborough.

All of this packing was then covered by ticking and made a pretty comfortable mattress, at least for the times.

When asked the price of seaweed, Mr. Scarborough replied, "I think the price at the time was about $20 on the local market and probably $30 delivered to the factory. A lot of times we would have to wait until my grandfather got his returns before we got paid. One time the money was so slow coming in and we had a bird around here that we called Wren at that time, and I remember making the remark that 'I wished that Wren would hurry and lay her eggs so I could get my money.' When Mr. Scarborough was 17 or 18, his uncle Walker, who owned a sailboat, made a trip once a week to Elizabeth City.

They carried the seaweed up and hauled freight back to the different villages on the way. They usually made the trip in a day, depending on the wind. They anchored off Chicamacomico, Waves, and Salvo, while boats rowed out to get groceries, drinks, and general merchandise.

KERRY HOOPER
HATTERAS MONITOR, NOVEMBER 1989

WINDMILLS

LEFT: *Kinnakeet Windmill* RIGHT: *Charles Williams II, with millstone used in the Bateman Miller Windmill*

In the early days, there were windmills in every village on Hatteras Island. The earliest known windmill (1723) was located in Kinnakeet, according to Ben Dixon McNeill and by other Hyde County records. These mills were called "post mills" because they were built on a central post; they had four blades, or sails, which were covered with canvas or cloth. The mill sat on a triangle-shaped frame of posts. The blades were slanted or angled to take advantage of prevailing wind conditions. The mills were used to grind the wheat and corn that was brought by the bushel from the mainland. Fishermen would take dried salted fish and shellfish to the mainland by boat and trade for wheat or corn to be ground into flour and cornmeal. Shellfish was not eaten at that time but was used as fertilizer for the mainland farms. Fish were plentiful at that time, so there was enough to eat with plenty left over to trade.

In the 1800s, there were two windmills in Kinnakeet. One was at the north end, at Mill Creek; the other at the south end, near where the mail boat landed. Belton Gray remembers that, when he was young, he and his father found the millstone and moved it from the shoreside to their home. The millstone in the accompanying photo is currently in Belton Gray's yard.

Records from Hyde County show that in 1824 Ezekiel Hooper sold a windmill to Pharoah Farrow. Ignatious Scarborough owned one of the mills in 1872. Later Bateman Miller was named as owner.

There was one windmill still standing in Kinnakeet in 1905. Windmills were also used as markers for navigation. They appear on many old maps.

BARBARA MEEKINS AUSTIN

George Oliver O'Neal of Avon (1883–1963) built perfect scale models of boats and had them on display in his general store. George Oliver O'Neal made this windmill from memory for Ben Dixon MacNeill. This windmill is a replica of the Bateman Miller windmill and is currently on display in the Smithsonian Museum, Washington, DC.

FRIENDS

BANKER CHILDREN

It would be surprising for children today
To see how we Banker children would play,
Simplest pleasures, entertainment was derived
With the few things at hand we improvised.

Paper dolls were my greatest passion,
Cutting pictures from catalogues of the latest fashion,
Sears, Spiegel, and Montgomery Ward
We were excited when new books arrived.

We cut out pictures for our families—
Mothers, fathers, children, and we
Spent hours playing out their experiences.
Their homes we fashioned and their furnishings.

If we ran out of catalogues, one would run out
To nearby Miss Willie's little outhouse
And, as toilet tissue was a luxury,
Folks used catalogues and they were free.

As stated above, one went to Miss Willie's
And soon returned with a valued handful
Of pictures that soon enlarged our collection.
Those were some of the happiest times of my recollection.

BROOKSIE MEEKINS KUHL

BANKER FRIENDS

These two photos show a group of Kinnakeeters who kept in touch with each other over the years. The first photo was taken in 1948 on the porch of Willie Ann Farrow's house in Avon Village. Willie Ann Farrow was Dallas Miller's grandmother.

The group got together in 2003 for a reunion photo. Both photos (l–r): Dallas Miller, Ronnie Price, Myrna King Robke, Barbara Meekins Austin, and Dennis Gray Hill.

COUSINS
(L–r): Mildred Williams Austin, Selma Gray Sterling, and Isabella Scarborough Gray

Lucy Farrow Miller, Nellie Midgett and Mildred Williams Austin

(L–r): Wallace Haywood, and Erving, Ellis, Wayne, and Larry Gray holding telescope from ship torpedoed off coast. Ship name and date unknown

FRIENDS
(L–r): Joe Williams, Nellie Midgett, Mildred Williams Austin, Lucy Farrow Miller, and Lorenzo Hooper

CAPE HATTERAS HIGH SCHOOL BUS DRIVERS, CIRCA 1961
Top (l–r): John Quidley, George Price, Roger Sutton, Shiela Gray, and McCray Riggs. Bottom (l–r): Wayland Jennette, JoAnne Wingate, Bertie Dixon, Dallas Miller, and I. G. Scarborough

FIFTH-GRADE STUDENTS
(L–r): Dallas Miller, Ann Meekins, Veda Gray, Helen Gray, Gail Gray, Mrs. Sue Williams (teacher), Ann Williams, and Donna Gray

AVON SCHOOL HOUSE, CIRCA MID-1950S

MEMORIES OF A BYGONE ERA

ON THE PORCH, AS TOLD BY LUCY FARROW MILLER

1931

It was Sunday, before church. Some friends and I were socializing on the front porch of the local store. He had joined the Coast Guard two years before, but was home for a visit. As he walked by he shouted to me, "Lucy, you look so pretty, I'd marry you." I remember the dress and hat I was wearing vividly. My uncle had taken me to Elizabeth City to get this Easter outfit and to have a perm put in my hair. This day was not Easter, but I still had the "look." That day, I didn't know how much Dallas would change my life.

MY ARRIVAL

In 1913, I was born on a cold day in the small island village of Little Kinnakeet, North Carolina. It was December 23, and everyone was preparing to celebrate the birth of Christ. My parents were John Divine and Willie Ann Farrow. I was the youngest of three girls, the oldest being Emma James and the middle, Dorcas Wilson. When I first arrived, my parents could not decide on the perfect name for me. It took several months before I became Lucy.

MY CHILDHOOD

Sisters Em, Dorcas, and I had a very happy life starting in Little Kinnakeet. We lived in a house that I still have behind the one I live in now. My mother's parents were Tilman and Lucinda Gray. Their home was next to ours on the north side. It was a two-story house with a porch in front, two bedrooms upstairs, and three rooms down—the living room with a fireplace, the kitchen, and another bedroom. The house was filled with memories. In the downstairs bedroom, there was a hole covered with a board. This is where a cannonball had been shot through during the painful Civil War. My mother's grandparents were Wallace and Cynthia Gray. This house belonged to them. Tilman was their only son, and he and Lucinda lived with them. The family owned much livestock—pigs, horses, cows, and sheep.

Since there was no running water at this time, some people had cisterns to catch the rainwater as it fell from the heavens. Some were made of cement and some built of wood. They were placed close to the house so it would be easy to dip into the water as needed. There also were wells dug in the sand. The men would dig until they reached water, then they would put barrels down into the hole so the sand could not reach the water. Next, they would put a high fence around it so nothing could get in the well. On the inside of the fence a hook was placed. There was a bucket with a string attached to it to hang on the hook. This was used to get the water. I can still recall how cool the water always stayed.

There was no electricity either. We used lamps filled with kerosene to light our homes. We were always warm because of the heat provided by the wood-burning stoves. These stoves were also used to cook some of the finest meals ever served. Hatteras was a wilderness. Until the late 1930s because there was no electricity, we had no refrigeration either.

My father's parents were Lancaster and Dorcas Farrow. Papa had three brothers and one sister. His sister and his brother George died when they were still small children. Then, while still a young boy, both his mother and father died. As a young man, he was in the Confederate Army. His youngest brother was Uncle Wilson. When Papa and Mama married, he came to stay with them. He never married and lived his entire life with us. Some say he is still with us in spirit.

My grandmother and great-grandmother did much handiwork. They made beautiful quilts by hand and did lots of intricate knitting. In my great-grandmother's backyard, there was a long table where the family men would put the sheep to shear. After the sheep were sheared, they were set loose to run any place they wanted to go. My grandmothers would wash the wool and spread it out to dry. They had something called cards to untangle the wool. These were two pieces about eight inches long and six inches wide, each having a handle at one end and bristles at the other. The wool was placed between one card on each hand. They would pull the wool until it was straight. Although I can picture this in my mind, I cannot summon up what it was called. It had a wheel and was worked by a pedal. After this step, a spinning wheel was used. This had a large wheel around which the thread went, and it also was worked by using a pedal. My great-grandmother kept all of the pieces in a bedroom on the second floor of her home. We children had great times going up there and playing with them. It was tremendous fun for us to pedal them and watch the wheels go around. In order to get brilliant colors, the women had to be creative. There was no dye to color the wool. There was a special wood that washed up on the shore that was purple. It looked as if it had been sawed from the limbs of trees rather than tossed out of the ocean. People boiled it to get the dye used on many different things. My grandmother dyed much wool with it. Perhaps that is why I still have such a fondness for the color purple.

There was a small church where everyone attended. The minister lived in the parsonage at Big Kinnakeet, a short distance away. He would drive a horse with cart or ride horseback to Little Kinnakeet to preach on Sundays. My father and a next-door neighbor, Nina Gray, always sang a special song. On weekdays, the church was used as a schoolhouse for lower grades. My oldest sister, Emma, taught there for a while. When reaching the higher grades, they had to go to school in Big Kinnakeet. Because of this, my father decided we should move there.

MY HAPPY TEENAGE YEARS

As a teenager, we did not have any of the amusement places like there are today. We had to create our own fun. We enjoyed ourselves doing a wide variety of different things. Our imaginations carried us many places.

The girls in Kinnakeet always had birthday parties, and girls and boys would attend. It would be at the birthday girl's house, and we would play games. I remember one of the games was "post office." In this, a boy would go inside a room and someone else would stand by the door. The boy in the room would say he had a letter for a particular girl, and the stander-by would tell the girl. She would then go inside the room and the boy would kiss her on the cheek. We felt real good when we were called. The prettiest girls were always first. After games, we were served home-baked cake with soda or lemonade for refreshment. Sometimes there was no ice in it. Since we did not have electricity, any ice came from the house where fish was packed. It didn't matter. We still had lots of fun. I remember the first boy who walked me home after one of these wonderful parties. We never dated, but he was a true friend.

Most every Sunday after we had gone to Sunday school and church, we came home and had dinner. This wasn't your typical lunch: it was a big Sunday dinner that would leave everyone satisfied. After dinner, many times the boys and girls would walk to the beach. We would sit on the sand hills and laugh and talk. We wore our dress-up clothes from church. One Sunday, a girl wore a beautiful hat. It was made of a lacelike material and had a wide brim collar that was tangerine colored. The wind blew it off her head and sent it toward the ocean. Luckily, one of the boys rescued it.

Dallas went in the United States Coast Guard when he was 17 years old. He said he was 21 to get in without his father's consent. He knew that it would provide a good life. After all, his father had been in the Life Saving Service. He only told the Coast Guard the truth about his age when he received information on applying for Social Security. Of course, he would not take this money until he was truly of age. When he joined the service, I was 15 years old. I only remember seeing him at one party. This was because we did not live close to each other. I really did not know that much about him. When he was away in the Coast Guard, he would write me letters. Being only 15, I never answered them. I would wonder why he was writing me. Now, of course, the reason is crystal clear.

INTERVIEW BY MICHELLE MILLER SMITH

LUCY'S FAMILY HOME

Located in Little Kinnakeet before the Life Saving Station was built, in the early 1920s the house was moved to the north end of Avon, where it is located today. In the downstairs bedroom, there was a hole covered with a board. This is where a cannonball had been shot from the Monticello *as it fired on Confederates fleeing north during the Civil War. The house was taken down piece by piece and brought to Avon by boat.*

FRONT LEFT: *Uncle Wilson Farrow holding Archie Meekins, John Walter Barnes, Euzelia Gray holding daughter Janet, Willie Ann Farrow holding June, Dorcas Farrow Meekins, Mary Tom Hooper sitting on porch, and Lucinda Gray standing on porch*

THE STORY OF FROGS

When I came along there were just about as many frogs in the village of Avon where I grew up as there were in Egypt when God brought the plague of frogs on the Egyptians so Pharaoh would let the Hebrew children go (as recorded in Exodus 8:1–4). When I was growing up, my father always had a garden, and he never had to use any pesticides to kill the worms and the bugs that got on his vegetables. The frogs ate them. We boys used to play with frogs, and we always had frog warts.

We lived near a pond, and those frogs in that pond at night during the summertime sounded like the Mormon Tabernacle Choir. They would make music like no one ever heard. Some of the words to their music in the far part of the night sounded as if they were saying, "Pull blanket, pull blanket, pull blanket." Then in the wee hours of the morning they would change their words that sounded as if they were saying, "Fry bacon, fry bacon, fry bacon," on and on again.

It used to amaze me how they would all start at the same time and stop at the same time. Only on certain occasions did the frogs ever sing by themselves. I wish someone had made a recording of those frogs.

Recently I had a cousin die at the age of 96. I called her Sis Em, and one of the things she asked me shortly before she fell and broke her hip and passed away was, "Herscal, do you ever see a frog?" She, too, always had a garden and depended on the frogs to keep the worms and the bugs picked off of her vegetables. I wish I could have found a frog, put it in a jar, and taken it to her to see. But I never did.

Well, do we ever think or wonder what has happened to the frogs? The last time I saw one, he was flat on the road, having been run over by a vehicle. So that may have been what inspired someone to write this little song that was in a brochure I recently received from one of our United

Methodist Children's Homes. It is titled "Tom the Toad" and is sung to the tune of "Oh, Christmas Tree." It goes like this:

Oh, Tom the toad,
Oh, Tom the toad
Why did you jump out in the road?
Oh, Tom the toad, Oh, Tom the toad, Why did you jump out in the road?
You were so big and green and fat
But now you're small and red and flat.
Oh, Tom the toad, Oh Tom the toad,
Why did you jump out in the road?

And that is the story of the frogs. And that is what one old man does when the snow has covered the ground and he cannot get out of the house and he comes down with cabin fever.

Shortly after I had written my story of the frogs, I was doing my usual walk in my neighborhood when a neighbor came running out to the road where I was walking and in a frantic voice said, "Mr. Williams, come here as quick as you can. The hot water hose to my washing machine has burst and my house is being flooded with water!"

Knowing I could not get to the washing machine to turn off the water because of the hot water coming out of the hose, I asked her to get the wrench that turned the water off at the meter box close to the street. She gave me the wrench, and when I removed the cover to the meter box, the place where I needed to put the wrench was covered with sand.

As I was removing the sand a big ol' frog leaped up on my arm. Well, I have never kissed a frog, but my first inclination was to do something that I had never done before!

HERSCAL P. WILLIAMS

POST OFFICE

The post office at Avon was established on December 4, 1873, with Dameron (Damon) T. Meekins as postmaster. The name was changed from Kinnakeet to Avon on March 22, 1883. Although no official record remains of why the post office selected the new name, it is speculated that it was named after medieval Stratford on Avon, a town in southwestern Warwickshire, in central England, on the Avon River: birthplace of William Shakespeare

We believe the first post office was located near the sound at the southern end of Kinnakeet, what is now called Benny's Landing. Mail was brought in by boat. A boat left Manteo in the morning, and it took all day to deliver mail down the island to Hatteras. A boat left Hatteras in the morning taking mail the other way. It was an all-day trip. The mail boat also carried some freight and passengers.

Gloria Williams O'Neal, daughter of Charles Williams, postmaster, sitting on the steps of the Avon Post Office located at the end of Williams Road, west of St. John UMC, 1936

When the mail boat came in, the postmaster or Tom Meekins would row out in a skiff taking outgoing mail and bringing in mail and any freight or passengers.

The post office was very small. Because there was no home delivery, you received your mail by walking up to the postmaster's window. This created a gathering place for locals to congregate and catch up on the latest news, gossip, and overall happenings within the community. Later the post office was enlarged and individual boxes were installed within the building, requiring a key for each individual family.

In 1897, the post office was moved to a lot across from the end of Williams Road, west of St. John United Methodist Church. Since then, it has been located just south of the old Cape Hatteras Hotel (on McMullen Road); from there, it moved to where the Subway now stands (where individual boxes were installed); then to the current location on Highway 12.

WAITING FOR THE MAIL BOAT TO COME IN

When I was coming along in the village of Avon back in the 1920s, there was very little overland transportation. Just about everything that came to the village came by sailboats. There were two sailboats. One was named the *Julia Belle,* which was owned by Farrow Scarborough, and the other by Loran O'Neal, which was named the *Missouri.* These boats were referred to as "freight boats," and they went to Elizabeth City once a week and brought their wares to Avon.

The *Julia Belle* also carried freight to Rodanthe, and the *Missouri* carried it to Buxton. There was also a mail boat that came to Avon from Manteo every day except Sunday bringing the mail. The boat left Manteo early in the morning and usually arrived at Avon around noontime.

Some time ago I read a story in *Readers Digest* about this fellow who grew up in West Virginia about the same time I did. He told how the only thing he had to do was go down to the train depot and wait for the train to come in. Well, we did not have a train depot, but a lot of us in the village of Avon went down to the landing by the Pamlico Sound and waited for the mail boat. That is how my poem "Waiting for the Mail Boat" came to be.

Years ago when times were bad
Not a cent of money was to be had.
For pastime and pleasure you and your friend
Went to the landing and waited for the mail boat to come in.

We never had a train depot
Where the trains would come and they would go.

We never saw a train coming round the bend
We just watched and waited for the mail boat to come in.

People would gather from all around
Hoping for a letter or package from some faraway town.
Sit there through the rain and the wind
Waiting by the shore for the mail boat to come in.

Folks would wait from noon to night.
Waiting for that mail boat to come in sight.
No one's day would ever end
Until that old mail boat had come in.

Then that mail boat would come close to the shore
Drop its anchor where it had dropped it before.
We would meet it with a smile and a grin.
For now that mail boat had come in.

HERSCAL P. WILLIAMS

THE GARDENER

There is a Kinnakeeter
Who constantly plants seed.
Not only does his seed produce food,
Souls he does feed.

He has planted, watered, and harvested
Many a fine crop;
But one problem seems to remain
From the bottom to the top.

You see these collards, tomatoes and "such"
Are full of many holes.
For creatures creep in to destroy
What God has intended to be pure food for souls.

But, in spite of all the imperfections, His harvest is known throughout the land.
It is the most delectable because it was planted
With loving, tender hands.

This kind of love dwells within the heart,
Not just shown on the face.

He is one who knows the Master
And experienced His grace.

The next time you see someone you may surmise
To be less than whole,
Do not be too quick to judge.
You may one day see them on the streets of gold.

Even in the midst of a crown of thorns
And a wooden cross,
Everlasting life has sprung forth
† Through the work of the gardener. †

LOIS GRAY MILLER, 2008

THE LEGEND OF THE DOGWOOD

The fable goes that the dogwood was once as tall as any tree in the forest. Because of its strength, the Romans chose it as the timber for the cross.

The tree felt great distress that it was to be put to such a cruel use. Jesus, nailed upon the cross, perceived the pity and sorrow of the dogwood and said, "Because of your sympathy for my sufferings, never again will the dogwood tree grow large enough to be used for a cross.

"Henceforth, the tree will be slender and bent. Each of its beautiful blossoms will grow four petals in the form of a cross. On the outer edge of each petal, there will be nail prints—brown with rust and stained with red. In the center of the flower, people will see a crown of thorns."

When you examine the dogwood blossom, I hope you will remember its lesson. I hope when, in your imagination, you "survey the wondrous cross," you will come away with the marvelous doctrine of the Resurrection. Jesus did not stay on the cross, nor did he stay in the tomb. He was raised from the dead to proclaim the victory of the Christian faith over death and defeat.

THE MASTER GARDENER

Say you have a garden, a beautiful garden with plants, flowers, and trees. You have taken care of this garden. You pulled the weeds, watered it when it needed water in dry seasons, picked up trash that blew in with the wind, pruned the plants and trees that needed pruning (cut away all the dead), and raked up all the fallen leaves.

What if things started happening that took your time away from the garden? It would not take long before weeds would be growing everywhere; the plants, trees, and flowers that you used to water would start to shrivel up and die; trash could blow in all over the garden. Soon it would not be a beautiful and peaceful place where you could go and rest and enjoy. What if you decided to take just a few minutes to run in and do a quick cleanup, because there are just too many other things that have your attention now. So you just cut down the weeds instead of pulling them up by the roots.

Months go by. You begin to miss the peaceful times you used to have in that beautiful garden. You walk out to the garden and you are aghast at what you see. The weeds and thorns have taken over and choked the life out of the beautiful plants. Now, instead of beauty, it looks so ugly in your garden. You rush in to try and do what you can. You can't pull the weeds up, the roots are too strong. The thorns and vines are hanging in your way. You realize you can't do this alone. You need a Master Gardener. This was not something you wanted to happen. It did not happen overnight. It took awhile.

The same thing can happen to the garden in our heart. If we neglect the negative things that come into our heart, over time the roots will grow strong and deep. Some of the things are bitterness, unforgiveness, hatred, anger, and so on. There may come a time that they are so strong and deep that we can't get rid of them ourselves, and we need the Master Gardener. His name is Jesus Christ. We will need to let Jesus come into the garden of our heart and do a work that will bring our garden back to being beautiful and peaceful. He knows how much to prune, and how to water, clear away debris, and get out the deep, strong roots. Once Jesus is finished with the work in our garden, it will once again be beautiful and peaceful—a garden that we will not be ashamed of—a place where we can sit or walk with Jesus and be at peace.

Lord Jesus, we ask You to look at our garden and see if there are any weeds, thorns, briars, or other things growing that do not please You. We ask You, Jesus, as the Master Gardener of our hearts, to come in and do the work that needs to be done so that You will see a beautiful, peaceful garden—a place that pleases You. Let our gardens all have beautiful fruit growing instead of weeds. We thank You and love You.

DARLENE SCARBOROUGH WILLIS
NEW LIVING TRANSLATION
1 PETER 5:8; MATTHEW 13:25; PHILIPPIANS 4:7; PROVERBS 4:2

THE FLOODS LIFTED UP

Having grown up on the coast of North Carolina, I have a special reverence and love for the ocean and the sounds that surround that part of the country. Some of my most wonderful (and a few of my most terrifying) memories are associated with the water. In either case, the power of God seems to echo in the sound of the waves.

As a small child, one of my favorite pastimes in the summer was playing along the water's edge. There was a particular strain of dark, gooey mud that was just right for molding dolls. My friends and I used to make our "families" and put them up on the banks to dry. As the sun beamed down, the figures baked hard as if they had been specially prepared. When life seems too harried, a deep calm can come over me as I relive those moments and hear the gentle sound of the waves rolling upon the shore. It is as if God is there bringing peace and serenity.

The power of God, however, is not always revealed in such a quiet way. Some of my most inescapable memories are of the violent storm of 1944 that destroyed our home and threatened the lives of relatives and friends. When I was 11 years old, I recall the fear I experienced as our extended family gathered at my grandparents' home, which was a safer location. We watched houses leaving their foundations as the sound and ocean met and the powerful winds and tide wreaked havoc. Yet I still remember the prayers of thanksgiving at the height of the storm when a huge house stopped just inches from ours as we prepared for the crash that the strong tide was bringing us.

The power of the mighty waves is awesome; however, the power of God is greater. My memories of the aftermath are not tales of woe and bitterness. They are of amazement and thanksgiving that no one was seriously injured. God had blessed the community. As the psalmist said, "The floods have lifted up."

When we are discouraged and problems arise, we sometimes wonder where God is. Yet we know He is mightier than "the thunder of many waters." Help us to see beyond the trials of today and realize that He is with us. Give us the calm that comes after a storm and be able to say Robert Browning's words:

> *God's in His Heaven—*
> *All's right with the world!*

MAXINE SCARBOROUGH THOMASSON

No soil upon earth is as dear to our eyes as the soil we first stirred in making mud pies.

AVON AERIAL AFTER 1944 HURRICANE
The Great Atlantic Hurricane of September 14, 1944, damaged approximately 96 of Avon's 115 houses. The houses were severely damaged or washed off their foundations by that storm. The idea of evacuation was unheard of at that time, thus many stories are told by the survivors.

I'm not afraid of storms, for I'm learning how to sail my ship.

LOUISA MAY ALCOTT

BYGONE DAYS AND EASTER BONNETS

Hats or bonnets are a form of headdress or head covering, especially one having a crown and brim. Hats serve several purposes: as ornaments, for protection, or to indicate status. They may not be in style anymore, but Christian women of a certain age recall the statement pieces once fashionable to don every Easter.

During the Victorian period, a lady's hat was a symbol of her wealth and social status. As communication across the nation improved, ideas and social standards could travel quickly. Rules of etiquette accompanied the wearing of the hat. A hat was required when out of doors or in public. When in the home, a simple cap or bonnet covered the head. Being hatless was acceptable only when grooming. Two major types of head coverings worn during the Victorian era were the hat and the bonnet. Bonnets initially had a large brim and a curtain of fabric (the bavolet) covering the neck. Hats had a crown and no bavolet. A hat may or may not have a brim. The hat developed into countless versions to suit the fashion of the day.

Ribbons, feathers, small stuffed animals, jewels, fabrics, and furs were used for hats. The demand for feathers caused the disappearance of several species of birds during the Victorian hat period. The Victorian lady adorned her hair with simpler versions of headgear for evening. Lovely beads, flowers, ribbons, and feathers were fashioned into jewels for the ornate hairstyles.

Into the 20th century, ladies' hats became simpler as the skirts got shorter and life got busier. By the 1920s untrimmed hats called cloches (a fitted, bell-shaped hat) became the uniforms for every woman. It was always worn well down over the eyes and represented the freedom and energy of the '20s. Spectator sports spurred the development of the simple hat of felt or straw. Fashion changed the shapes rapidly during the '20s. In retrospect, the most vibrant era of millinery seems to be the Victorian period when the extravagant use of lovely materials topped the heads of ladies of all walks of life. It isn't just bonnets that went out of fashion. Go to church these days and female parishioners haven't just abandoned bonnets; they're often wearing casual slacks—even shorts—instead of dresses.

Hats and bonnets are a fun part of our fashion history! Where are the little girls in frilly new dresses and bonnets, and does anyone have an Easter bonnet anymore?

There's the fancy hat and frilly dress! Photo of Lucy, Dallas, and granddaughter Michelle Miller

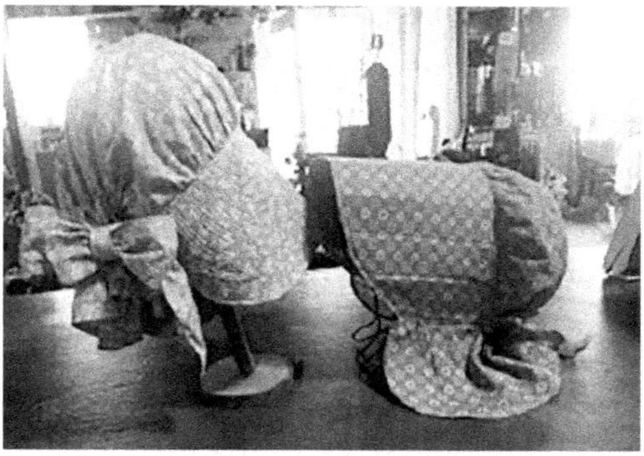

Bonnets of Martha W. Gray (left) and Lucinda Farrow Gray (right)

Martha Williams Gray clamming on soundside in Avon, wearing her bonnet for protection from the sun

PAINTING BY BROOKSIE MEEKINS KUHL

Fields and Menville Meekins. Grandma Menville loved her hats and bonnets.

MEMORIES OF 1926 EVENT STIRRED WITH APPROACH OF 18TH OF AUGUST

As we approach August 18, when the people of Dare County commemorate the birth of the first English child born in America, I am reminded of that date back in 1926 when one of the first celebrations was held in Manteo.

I had a great-uncle who was a retired Methodist minister by the name of Andrew Price, who owned a boat that was referred to as a skipjack. Several teenagers from the village of Avon approached my uncle to take them on his boat to Manteo for this event. My uncle agreed and went to great length in getting the boat ready for the trip. I was eight years old at the time. My mother went along and took my sister Jeanie and myself, as my brother Alton was part of the crew of the Coast Guard Cutter *Pamlico* and the *Pamlico* was bringing the ambassador of Great Britain to Manteo for the celebration.

On the morning of August 17 we set sail from Avon. The wind was blowing a pretty good breeze from the southwest. When we were approximately eight miles into the trip, one of the teenagers, Burgess Gray, asked my uncle if he could steer the boat. To steer the boat, there was an iron rod known as a tiller approximately three feet in length attached to the rudder.

My uncle agreed to let Burgess steer the boat. My uncle had been sitting on the deck to steer, but Burgess wanted to stand, so he fastened a line around the end of the tiller. As stated, the wind was blowing a pretty stiff breeze from the southwest. Keeping the boat on course required keeping some strain on the tiller.

My mother and I were standing at the doorway of the cabin of the boat. The doorway was facing the stern, and we were watching Burgess steer the boat. All at once the line came off the tiller and Burgess fell overboard. We were in what is known as the Gull Shoal Channel, and the water was very deep. My uncle immediately took hold of the tiller and turned the boat up in the wind and immediately one of the teenagers on the boat, Watson Gray, who was in his early or middle teens, pushed a small skiff, which was on the deck of the boat, over the side and began shoving the skiff to where Burgess was.

I remember seeing the paddle Watson was using to shove the skiff. The water was so deep that only a small part of the paddle was above the water, and he was shoving against the wind. But in a short period of time, Watson reached Burgess and pulled him out of the water and got him in the small skiff.

He brought Burgess, who was unconscious, to the boat, placed him on the deck, and two or three of those on board the boat used artificial respiration. Burgess was soon revived. Later on he came back to the stern of the boat and began steering the boat again.

We proceeded to Manteo and on the next day, August 18, 1926, somehow

The G. H. O'Neal. *A replica of a skipjack boat made by L. P. O'Neal. A skipjack was a fishing boat and was the last working boat under sail in the United States.*

we went to the north end of Roanoke Island, where the ambassador from Great Britain was brought ashore in a small boat from the Coast Guard Cutter *Pamlico,* and my brother Alton was in the boat as well.

I would like to add that during our stay in Manteo we stayed with a lady from Avon, Mrs. Jodie Williams, whose husband was in the Nags Head Coast Guard Station, and it was here, I remember, I ate my first hamburger and drank my first glass of iced tea. What an occasion!

HERSCAL WILLIAMS SR.
THE COASTLAND TIMES, AUGUST 17, 2003

FRESH LIVING WATER

While visiting Kinnakeet as a child, I was amazed at the freedom and safety to roam the village with cousins and friends. On a hot summer day, water was plentiful because cisterns were a part of the homes throughout the village. A cistern was a large container made of wood or cement that was used to collect water.

You could always find a dipper with a handle to help yourself to a cool drink from a cistern. Because of modern technology, cisterns are scarce today, but some of the historical houses still have cisterns in place but not used. When you pass Chicamacomico Life Saving Station in Rodanthe, North Carolina, you can see a cistern next to the old Life Saving Station.

Cisterns catch and store rainwater much like in ancient biblical days, except the cisterns of the Bible were normally covered pits carved out of rock to store water. The prophet Jeremiah talked about the drought of Jerusalem. The nobles send their servants for water; they go to the cisterns but find no water. They return with their jars unfilled; dismayed and despairing. Israel had forsaken God, and the Word of the Lord came to Jeremiah,

saying, "'My people have committed two sins: They have forsaken me, the spring of living water, and have dug their own cisterns, broken cisterns that cannot hold water'" (Jeremiah 2:13).

In abandoning God, they had traded a gushing spring for a leaking cistern. It was evident that they were trusting in themselves instead of God. But the disciple John (John 4:13) shares the story of Jesus telling the Samaritan woman about living water. He told her, "Everyone who drinks this water I give him will never thirst. Indeed, the water I give him will become in him a spring of water welling up to eternal life. This is living water—fresh flowing spring water, not stagnant water."

Cisterns symbolized security in the Old Testament, but God has a greater plan for us today. His name is Jesus, and He fills us with *fresh living water* that is called *the Holy Spirit*. Is your source of living water dripping, or is it a steady stream?

LOIS GRAY MILLER

AFTERNOON DELIGHTS

AFTERNOON DELIGHTS, SOUTHERN STYLE

Rebecca Wallace Williams Scarborough (1883–1916), Avon (Kinnakeet), North Carolina

FAVORITE AFTERNOON RECIPES FROM THE OUTER BANKS OF NORTH CAROLINA

Within the following pages you will find recipes and features that are a part of the tradition of hospitality so well known in the South. We do not claim all of these recipes to be original but are authentic heirloom recipes shared by many Outer Bankers and are reminiscent of a bygone era.

LOIS GRAY MILLER

DINNER AT LITTLE KINNAKEET LIFEBOAT STATION

In as much as this report has something to do with the culinary arts and Kinnakeet, it seems only fair that I share a very pleasant experience I recall that centers around the Little Kinnakeet Lifeboat Station and crew members during one of my visits.

It was during the summer of 1925 or maybe 1926. My father, George Harrison Meekins, was officer-in-charge at Little Kinnakeet and, after some persistent begging on my part, consented to let me spend the night at the station. A time away from my home in Avon was exciting. I was 10 years old at the time and enjoyed being around older men, especially those serving as crew members at this station. The trip up the beach was made in my dad's 1925 Ford Model T.

Dad and I arrived at the station just before 4 p.m. Supper was always on the table at that time of day. Dorther Gray was cook, so during the meal he said, "Boys, what are we going to have for dinner [noon meal] tomorrow?" After considering navy beans, collard greens, canned string beans, etc., it was decided that a meal of stewed fish would be great. My dad, being quite a hunter and set net fisherman, agreed to be the one to get the fish. I was excited at the thought of going in the sound with him. So, after supper we walked down the station landing path to the sound, Pamlico Sound, and loaded several nets on board a small shove skiff. The nets had been hanging on what was referred to as "net racks" to assure drying after being used. Nets in those days were made from cotton thread and would rot if put away wet. We set off in a northwesterly direction toward an area of white bottom. Net setting was completed about sunset, and Dad decided to stay by the nets and fish them a bit longer, after "sunset down." This term was used to identify the period after sunset when all the pink glow from the day's sun disappeared, usually around 9 p.m. There was no such thing as Daylight Saving Time.

When the proper time arrived, Dad said, "Son, let's fish down 'em." We started checking the nets, picking out small croakers and an occasional spot. Suddenly he said, "Boy, we've caught a nice sunfish [pompano]." While he was carefully easing the sunfish toward the side of the skiff, I, in great excitement, grabbed the net to help and, in doing so, caused the fish to free itself from the net and escape, lost! I vividly remember Dad uttering something like "dag gonnet." I never heard him use profanity. A sunfish was considered a delicacy and not often caught in a small mesh net.

We finished and proceeded back toward shore, Dad using a "shoving paddle" to propel the skiff. Outboard motors would come some years later.

The next morning before daybreak, Dad aroused me from a deep sleep, telling me, "Come. Let's go fish the nets." We finished the nets, returned to shore, carried the catch back to the station, and ate breakfast. After breakfast some of the crew began the task of cleaning the fish in preparation for dinner. They were scaled, eviscerated, and the head and tail removed.

When it came time to start cooking the noon meal, Mr. Dorther, using a large iron pot, sat the pot on the iron wood-burning stove, put a large amount of sliced salt pork inside, and proceeded to fry out the pork. He then cut the small croakers in two pieces and at the same time peeled and cut Irish potatoes in large chunks. He put water in the pot, sifted a large amount of pepper and salt, and cooked the potatoes for a few minutes along with cut-up onions. After a short while he dumped the fish in the pot, along with cornmeal dumplings and green onion, and stood by while the cooking took place. Mr. Dorther didn't seem to mind me watching.

At about 11:30 the dinner bell was rung, and the crew began leaving the main station building and walking across the yard to the "cook house." Those present were all older men: Uncle Shank Meekins, Mr. Bembry Miller, Mr. Joe "Merry" Williams, Mr. Nelson Gray, Mr. Alonzo Gray, Mr.

Graves Midgette, Seymour Gray, Dad—and me. The man who manned the lookout tower on top of the main station building ate later.

Dad took a seat on the west end of the long table, and I sat on the southwest corner, in a place usually occupied by the crew member who was on annual leave or on liberty.

All ate with gusto, taking portions from large plates placed in the center of the table. The plates would be slid back and forth, the nearest man helping himself. Coffee was the beverage. I can't remember anyone drinking anything but coffee.

The most impressionable thing I remember about this feast was the large pile of bones beside each plate—and another thing: I can't remember seeing anything like a napkin available on the table.

MANSON MEEKINS, 2003 (AGE 87)

Lots of history in this photo! Manson Meekins returning home to Kinnakeet after World War II and being greeted by his mother, Omie Meekins, and niece Judy Gray Scarborough. Manson is wearing an officer's USCG gray uniform. This uniform was worn from 1943 through 1949. In the background is a water tower located on Willie Gray's property, on Methodist Church Road. Willie provided his family with water from his own water tower generated by a Delco motor.

TEA

A story handed down generation to generation gives credit for the discovery of tea to Chinese emperor Shen Nung, a man concerned with matters of health and wellbeing. He had observed that people who boiled water before drinking it suffered less from sicknesses, so he incorporated the extra step into his daily routine.

The story continues that one day, around 2737 BC, the emperor used wood from an evergreen plant, *Camellia sinensis*, for building a fire to heat water. When the wind blew, a few leaves from the wood fell into the pot, a wonderful aroma enticed the emperor to drink the resulting liquid, and tea was discovered. The first mention of tea in literature was around AD 350 in China. By 1658, Thomas Garway had advertised the properties of tea from his coffeehouse in London as "the excellent and by all physitians approved China drink, called by the Chineans Tcha, by other nations Tay, alias tea."

Portuguese merchants, with established trade routes to the Far East, are credited with bringing tea leaves to Lisbon. From Portugal, Dutch traders introduced the hot, fragrant drink to other European countries, and England, where the very wealthy quickly adopted the beverage. It is said that Catherine of Braganza, wife of Charles II, brought tea as a part of her dowry from her homeland of Portugal and introduced the drink at court. What had begun in England as a luxury for the upper class eventually became the national drink in Great Britain by the mid- to late 1600s. The Dutch established direct trade with the Orient, forming the Dutch East India Company, and tea became more affordable to those outside the gentry class. The practice of serving tea with food, in the afternoon between meals, is generally thought to have originated with Anna,

Duchess of Bedford, who initiated the practice to ward off "sinking spells." At that time, meals consisted of a large breakfast, a light lunch, and a large dinner served around 8 or 9 p.m.

The idea gained popularity and became known as afternoon tea. Tea was exported to the colonies by 1650, and in the New World, the custom of tea drinking became as popular as in England. Tea time became an opportunity to entertain, to display genteel manners, and to associate with other members of society.

LUCY'S KINNAKEET YAUPON TEA

Have you ever tasted yaupon tea? Have you ever decorated your house with yaupon, a member of the holly family? The tradition of yaupon tea—black drink or *Ilex vomitoria*—dates back many years. Early American Indians used it as a ceremonial beverage, believing it was a sign of purity. It was drunk mainly by adult males of high social standing. These coastal Carolina Indians accredited yaupon tea with being a cure for smallpox, kidney stones, diabetes, and even alcoholism.

The people of Kinnakeet (Avon) were best known for making "the strong drink," and at one time the tea provided a means of industry for the locals, who prepared it and exported it to the mainland. By the 1890s, drinking yaupon tea, a favorite of the locals, was scorned as a rural habit, and "yaupon eaters" became a derogatory term for referring to coastal people. There are a number of stories about how this phrase developed. One story is told that the supporters of a rival baseball team invented the jeer "Kinnakeeters, yaupon eaters" directed toward the people of Kinnakeet, and the phrase became fighting words for many years to come. The name Kinnakeet was changed to Avon in 1883 by the post office department.

Eventually, the tradition of yaupon tea became nearly extinct, with very few knowing the preparation process. The Native American heritage was the drying of yaupon to make tea. You must not only use the leaves but also the twigs because the twigs give it a sweet taste. The yaupon is gathered and parched—or "sweated," as it was called. The parched yaupon was boiled in water and the plant yielded a dark tea. For a modern version of the tea, gather the yaupon leaves and twigs and chop, next roast, in an iron skillet in the oven at 350 degrees until the leaves are browned.

Remove the yaupon from the oven and add ¼ cup of the yaupon to 3 cups of water in a pan. Place on top of the stove and bring to a boil. Simmer 10 to 12 minutes, then strain and serve. Store the remaining tea leaves in the refrigerator. Later, they may be added to 2 cups water and reused.

SOUTHERN SWEET TEA

Our lifestyle has changed significantly since the Victorian Era, but our taste buds still savor the refreshing taste of tea. In the South, sweet tea seems to be the drink of choice. From yaupon tea served in the 1800s to our modern teas, we still struggle with the ingredients to make the perfect tea.

Recently while dining in Washington, DC, my friends and I ordered "sweet tea," only to be told by the waitress that we were not quite far enough south to order "sweet tea." You see, sweet tea is the DNA test for southern family identity.

So what's the big secret to sweetened tea? Just add sugar to hot tea! Like any southerner we want sweetened tea with our meal, so began the quest to figure the appropriate ingredients for sweetened tea.

We never measure. We put the sugar in the pitcher, add the brewed tea to the pitcher, and somehow it always comes out just right. But for those who feel a need for the recipe, here goes:

6 regular-sized tea bags
2 quarts water
¾ cup sugar

Brew 6 tea bags with water in a teapot or other small pot. Pour sugar into a 2-quart pitcher, add hot tea to the sugar, and stir. Do not use a glass pitcher.

Love and scandal are the best sweeteners of tea.

HENRY FIELDING

THE ORIGIN OF THE SANDWICH

The modern sandwich is named after Lord Sandwich, but the exact circumstances of its invention and original use are still the subject of debate. A rumor in a contemporary travel book called *Tour to London* by Pierre Jean Grosley formed the popular myth that bread and meat sustained Lord Sandwich at the gambling table. A very conversant gambler, Lord Sandwich did not take the time to have a meal during his long hours playing at the card table. Consequently, he would ask his servants to bring him slices of meat between two slices of bread, a habit well known among his gambling friends. Because John Montagu was the Earl of Sandwich, others began to order "the same as Sandwich"—thus, the sandwich was born. In English, before the term "sandwich" was applied to sandwiches, they were just referred to as "bread and meat" or "bread and cheese."

LUCY'S TUNA SALAD FOR SANDWICHES

2 potatoes or more, depending on how many are being served
1 can tuna fish, approximately 12-ounce can, drained
1 Tablespoon onion, diced
salt and pepper to taste
mayonnaise

Peel and dice potatoes, place in pot of water, and boil until tender.
Remove from stove and drain.
Mash potatoes until there are no lumps.
Drain tuna and add to potatoes.
Add onion.
Add salt and pepper.
Add mayonnaise to moisten above ingredients.

In the olden days, salad was made from availability of fish. Many times the fish was left over from a dinner of baked or boiled fish and made into a salad for a sandwich for lunch the next day.

KINNAKEET PIEBREAD (DUMPLINGS)

2 cups flour (not self-rising)
1 teaspoon salt
⅔ cup very warm water, but not boiling

Measure dry ingredients into bowl and stir thoroughly to blend.

Make a well in the dry ingredients and add water, a little at a time. Stir with fork or knead with hand until mixture rolls up in a ball and no dry ingredients remain. If it is too sticky add a little flour; if it is crumbly, add a little water. It's important to knead until this dough works into a ball, about 5 minutes.

Shape dough into small balls and sprinkle with a small amount of flour.

Let the dough set for several hours, covered. You can even make your piebread and let it set all day, or if in a hurry, mix just before you make the stew.

There are several ways to place the piebread into the pot. Several suggestions are listed below:

1. Stretch each small ball by hand and place individually in the pot.
2. Dust a surface with flour, roll dough with a rolling pin.
3. Stretch and then roll the dough.

When adding piebread to pot, add one piece at a time, rotating from one side of the pot to the other so it will not stick together.

Put a layer of chicken, then a layer of piebread; continue in this order until all of the chicken is used. The layering prevents the piebread from clumping together. Piebread is used for many different types of stews, such as crab, beef, pork chop, and yes, even fowl such as goose.

Piebread is a trial-and-error type of recipe: If you don't succeed, try and try again, or better yet, call a Kinnakeeter and get them to walk you through this process. Every family does it differently.

VINTAGE RECIPES

Old Little Kinnakeet Recipes by Menvil Meekins

CRACKLING BREAD

1 cup cracklings, cubed
1 cup buttermilk
½ teaspoon soda
¼ cup flour
1 ½ cups cornmeal
¼ teaspoon salt

Cracklings: When you kill a hog, save some of the pork fat after lard has been rendered from it. Cut into cubes and fry in frying pan until crisp and brown. Remove cubes from pan.

Mix dry ingredients. Add milk. Stir in cracklings. Form into rolls and place in pan.

Bake 30 minutes at 400 degrees.

STEWED CHICKEN

Kill chicken. Hang up, let blood drip for a while. Scald and remove feathers. Singe to remove all feathers left. Cut up chicken. Soak in salt water. Rinse well.

Cover with water, add salt and pepper. Stew until almost tender. Then add potatoes and dumplings (using your favorite recipe).

In this modern day, it is not necessary to prepare the chicken. You simply go to the grocery store and purchase the chicken, which is ready to cook.

STEWED CHICKEN: A MORE MODERN VERSION (CHICKEN AND DUMPLINGS)

5-pound chicken, cut in pieces (if you prefer only white meat, just use chicken breast)
4 potatoes, peeled and cut in half, or just several large potatoes (potatoes optional)
salt and pepper to taste
water to cover

Make piebread and set aside. (Recipe for piebread is on page 194.)

Place chicken in stew pot. Add water to cover chicken and bring to boil. Let simmer for approximately 20 minutes before placing potatoes in pot (optional). When the chicken is tender, remove it from the pot, then add piebread. Place layer of piebread and then layer of chicken; continue until you use all of the chicken. If more bread remains, place pieces around edges of pot and on the top of stew. Add salt and pepper. Cook on medium and do not put lid tightly on pot because it will have a tendency to boil over onto the stove.

Cook until chicken and potatoes are tender to the touch, approximately 15 minutes. You may have to add more water—but not much, or the gravy will be too watery. If you find that the stew is too watery, add 2 Tablespoons of flour mixed in ¼ cup of water to help thicken it.

> There is no spectacle on earth more appealing than that of a beautiful woman in the act of cooking dinner for someone she loves.
>
> THOMAS WOLFE

CLAM CHOWDER

1 pint clams with juice, chopped
2 medium potatoes, cubed
1 small onion, chopped
¼ cup salt pork, diced
salt and pepper to taste
water to cover

Add water to cover ingredients.

In a medium saucepan, fry salt pork until brown and crispy. Add onion and sauté until tender but not brown. Add clams and their liquid. Add remaining ingredients; simmer until done (potatoes should be tender).

Yield: 2 servings.

> Honour to Womankind! Its needs must be that God loved Woman since He fashioned Thee.
>
> CHRISTINE DE PISAN, 1429

Dallas B. Miller

OYSTER SOUP

¼ cup salt pork, diced
1 teaspoon cornmeal
1 quart oysters, shucked (reserve the liquid)
salt and pepper to taste
water to cover

In a large saucepan, fry salt pork until brown and crispy.

Mix meal with a small amount of warm water in a cup. Stir and add to saucepan. Add oysters, liquid, salt, pepper, and enough water to cover. Bring to boil. Cover and remove from heat. Serve with cornbread or fritters.

Dallas B. Miller

BAKED FISH—SHEEPSHEAD, FLOUNDER, OR DRUM

3 to 4 pounds (at least) sheepshead, flounder, or drum
4 strips salt pork or bacon
8 potatoes, diced
1 large onion, sliced
salt and pepper to taste
water

Score the fish. Scoring lets heat circulate around the flesh for quick, even cooking. To score make parallel incisions with a sharp knife through the skin and flesh of the fish. Score approximately 2 inches apart between the fin and tail, depending on size of fish.

Salt and pepper scored fish.

Place fish in a large roasting pan or baking dish. Place salt pork or bacon strips on top of the fish.

Arrange potatoes and onion around the fish. Sprinkle salt and pepper onto the potatoes and onions. Add water to mid-level of pan and bake at 350 degrees for 30 to 45 minutes until fish appears to be done. Fish is done when the flesh is white.

THE FLOUNDER EXPERIENCE

Since I am enjoying a class that has inspired me to a new level of appreciation for all that is creation, allow me to share with you a recipe requiring an excursion. Of course, for less adventurous souls, I am sure a trip to the grocery store will suffice. Let's begin.

If you've never been flounder-gigging, let me tempt you into a new hobby. Picture, if you will, a pipe with a slightly curved end that is an oversized flashlight for your dark and mysterious ocean tour. Don't worry about the waves, you'll be venturing through the sound-side's still waters. Here you will spot small sharks, all sorts of rays, fish, jellies, and with any luck some nicely sized flounders soundly sleeping. If you're there to actually gig one, this is where you aim your spear and make sure not to hit any toes. I'd aim just above the gills to ensure a beautiful fillet.

My grandfather (Collins Gray Sr.) was usually full of wise advice and cautionary tales, so it behooves me to warn you that you want to wear shoes. You don't absolutely have to, of course, but no one likes a stray fish hook or sliver of shell in their heel. It really holds the potential of ruining your excursion.

You'll also want to do this little adventure in true disciplelike manner: in pairs. Be sure to choose someone much slower than yourself to ensure you can adequately outrun them in the emergency of a larger breed of shark. If that's not possible, then be sure to pray before descending the beach and choose someone with a compassionate soul; carry the spear. While on the topic of keeping excellent company, you should know that is what makes this event so very special. You will experience a bond here like none other. You and your partner may go into the waters as sacrifice and athlete, but you will emerge united by creation.

I'm pulling your leg about the scariness of the dark waters, though it is a rush for a homebody like myself. This is a wondrous thing to do with friends, and I highly recommend you try it one day. Just be sure to take extra batteries for your flashlight.

As for your catch, there is no secret to uncover when it comes to fried fish fillets. Simply toss the fillet in some House Autry and throw into hot oil until browned and crispy. Kinnakeet-style fried fish has no liquid dredge to keep a thin crispy outer coating, and we like our fish killed twice.

CHARLOTTE GRAY DAVISON, 2018

OLD-FASHIONED BEAN SOUP

1 pound dry navy beans (other dry beans such as black-eyed peas or lima beans may be cooked the same way)
2 quarts water
1 pound ham on bone or 1 pound salt pork
1 teaspoon salt
½ teaspoon pepper
2 bay leaves

Place washed beans in a large pot with 2 quarts water. Add remaining ingredients and cook on medium for 2 to 3 hours or until desired tenderness.

CORN BREAD OR CORN FRITTERS

(Kinnakeeters Call Them "Flitters")

1 cup all-purpose flour
¼ cup sugar
4 teaspoons baking powder
¾ teaspoon salt
1 cup cornmeal
2 eggs
1 cup milk
¼ cup shortening or melted butter

Mix flour with sugar, baking powder, and salt; stir in cornmeal. Add eggs, milk, and shortening. Beat about 1 minute.

Pour into greased 9x9 pan. Bake at 425 degrees for 20 to 25 minutes.

This recipe may also be used to make fritters or flitters. Mix all ingredients in a medium bowl. Heat ½ to 1 cup Crisco shortening in iron skillet. Drop spoonfuls of batter into skillet, then cook until air bubbles appear and fritters are golden brown. Turn and brown the other side. Serve with seafood or beans.

> To read about a country's cuisine isn't simply to go looking for "good things"; it is also to better know by means of the recipes the customs and richness or poverty of a place, and the spirit of those who inhabit it. It is, above all, to participate in the symbolic celebration of the shared repast.
>
> GINETTE OLIVESI-LORENZIAS

PONE BREAD

2 cups cornmeal
⅓ cup all-purpose flour
⅓ cup molasses
⅓ cup sugar
½ teaspoon baking soda
½ teaspoon salt
1 quart hot or boiling water

Mix cornmeal and flour with hot water. Cover and let set overnight. The next morning add remaining ingredients. Generously grease an iron skillet and place in oven to melt the grease. Place ingredients in frying pan and bake at 350 degrees for approximately 45 minutes to 1 hour. Let cool before serving.

> To boyle EGGS
> A certayne and infallible method to boyle new laid eggs so as to sup up and yet that theye have the white turned to milk is this. Break a very little hole at the bigger end of the shell, and put it into water while it boyleth. Let it remain boyling whiles your Pulse beateth two hundred Stroakes. Then take it out immediately, and you will find it of an exact temper.
>
> COOKERY BOOK OF THE 17TH CENTURY

ISABELLA'S WATERMELON RIND PICKLES

1 large watermelon rind, cut into squares
salt
alum
vinegar
water to cover
pickling spice

Select a melon with thick, tender rind. Cut off thick green skin and remove pink pulp. Cut rind in squares, wedges, or fancy shapes with a crinkle French-fry cutter or by hand.
Sprinkle salt over watermelon rinds and let soak in salt bath overnight.

Rinse rind and pack into sterilized pint jars.
Sprinkle pinch of alum on top of rind.
Pour equal amounts of vinegar and water into jars.
Add 1 teaspoon pickling spice to each jar and seal.

Refrigerate for approximately 3 days before eating.

This is a very simple recipe in which you can substitute cucumbers for the watermelon rind.

Wash cucumbers, cut into spears, and place in jars, any size, then add ingredients listed above.

This is a tangy pickle, not sweet.

> October 12 was originally known as Queen Isabella Day, now known as Columbus Day. He sailed the boat, but it was the lady who came up with the cash.

MELTING CHOCOLATE IN A MICROWAVE

CHOCOLATE SQUARES

Place them still in their wrappers with the seam side up on a plate and microwave on medium for 1 minute per square. Use a spatula to slide the chocolate into a mixing bowl, and you'll have no pan to clean up.

CHOCOLATE CHIPS

Melt with little chance of scorching in a microwave, eliminating the need for a double boiler. One half to 1 cup of chips will take 3 to 4-½ minutes to melt on medium heat or 70 percent power.

Stir after melting until mixture is smooth.

DO YOU WANT CHOCOLATE FONDUE WITH A KICK?

Melt 12 ounces of semisweet chocolate chips and ½ cup heavy cream over medium-low heat. Stir in 1 teaspoon vanilla and 1-½ teaspoons Tabasco brand pepper sauce. That's right, Tabasco sauce.

CHOCOLATE CHESS PIE

1 stick margarine (room temperature)
1 cup sugar
2 eggs, beaten
¼ cup cocoa
1 teaspoon vanilla
¼ teaspoon salt
1 9-inch pie shell

Whip margarine and sugar.
Blend in other ingredients.
Pour into 9-inch uncooked pie shell.
Bake at 325 degrees for 30 minutes.

REBECCA'S CHOCOLATE BREAD PUDDING

9 rolls bread (approximately): homemade, loaf, or burger rolls
1 Tablespoon butter or margarine
2 cups sugar
1-½ cups evaporated milk
1 Tablespoon vanilla

Soak bread in water until soft, drain as much water from bread as possible.

Mash bread.

Mix ½ cup plus 2 or 3 Tablespoons cocoa.

Taste test for sweetness. Bake at 400 degrees for approximately 40 minutes.

CHOCOLATE LAYERED COCONUT BARS, MEANT FOR MICHELLE

1 box confectioner's sugar (powdered sugar)
5 Tablespoons Crisco shortening (not oil)
¼ teaspoon vanilla flavoring
5 Tablespoons fresh milk (not canned)
½ cup coconut (more if desired)
1 12-ounce bag semi-sweet chocolate bits*

Mix all ingredients except chocolate bits.

This mixture is very thick; if you have trouble mixing it by hand, use a food processor. Melt semi-sweet chocolate bits in microwave oven for 3-½ minutes (cook control 70 percent power).

Grease an 8x9-inch pan or baking dish.

Spread soft layer of chocolate over bottom of container, approximately ⅛th-inch thick.

Pat out a layer of sugar mixture and lay over chocolate, about same thickness. Add another layer of soft chocolate. Be careful not to stir chocolate into sugar layers. Pat another layer of sugar mixture and spread on chocolate.

When finished, there should be three layers of chocolate and two layers of sugar mixture.

Check consistency of chocolate frequently until it is firm enough to cut. Do not wait until it is hard.

As soon as it is firm enough to cut, cut into small pieces and leave until completely hardened. Chocolate will return to the same consistency as before the melting process.

**Mint extract may be added to chocolate for variety in taste.*

In 1920, the Nineteenth Amendment was passed. Women were allowed the right to vote.

LUCY'S COCOA FUDGE

⅔ cup Hershey's Cocoa
3 cups sugar
⅛ teaspoon salt
1-½ cups evaporated milk
4-½ Tablespoons butter
1 Tablespoon vanilla

Combine cocoa, sugar, and salt in a large saucepan. Add milk, bring to boil, stirring frequently. Cook on low until a small amount of mixture forms a soft ball when dropped in cold water (approximately 30 minutes). Remove from heat, drop in butter, and cool to lukewarm (approximately 20 minutes). Add vanilla, beat until thick, and pour in buttered pan.

I use full-strength evaporated milk. I let it start boiling and boil 30 minutes, take it off the stove, add butter or margarine, and let it cool. Then beat until it loses the glossy look and pour in buttered pan.

DREAM BARS

Crust:
1 cup all-purpose flour
½ cup granulated sugar
½ cup (1 stick) margarine

Topping:
2 eggs, beaten
1 cup brown sugar
2 Tablespoons flour
½ teaspoon baking powder
1 teaspoon vanilla
¼ teaspoon salt

2 cups (12-ounce package) semi-sweet chocolate morsels

For crust: Combine flour and sugar in medium bowl.
Cut in margarine until mixture resembles coarse crumbs.
Press firmly and evenly onto bottom of a greased 9x12-inch pan.
Bake in preheated oven at 350 degrees until slightly brown.

For topping: Combine dry ingredients, add eggs (beat well), and add chocolate morsels.
Spread over crust.
Bake in 350-degree oven for 20 to 25 minutes or until golden brown.
Cut into squares.

Makes about 2-½ dozen bars.

For variation: Spread your favorite jam over hot crust and then add topping and morsels; continue with recipe.

LORENE'S 10-LAYER CHOCOLATE CAKE

1 box butter-flavored cake mix
1 stick margarine
3 large eggs
1 teaspoon vanilla
1-¼ cup water (½ cup to begin)

Mix ½ cup water with remaining ingredients in a mixing bowl. Add remaining water to batter and mix well.

Grease and flour 8- or 9-inch cake pans. This recipe makes 10 thin layers, so you will need to reuse your cake pans. Put small piece of wax paper on bottom of each pan.

Put approximately ⅔ cup batter in each pan, spreading with back of spoon. Bake in a preheated 350-degree oven for 10 minutes.

All layers should be cooled before frosting.

LORENE'S 10-LAYER CHOCOLATE CAKE ICING

2 cups sugar
2 sticks margarine
7 ounces evaporated milk
1 12-ounce package semi-sweet chocolate chips
2 cups miniature marshmallows

In a 3-quart saucepan, add the sugar, margarine, and milk; bring to boil. Boil for 5 minutes (does not require stirring).

Remove from heat and add chocolate chips, stirring until almost melted. Add marshmallows and stir until melted.

Cool 3 to 4 hours or until thick and then frost cake.

GRANDMA MARY OBBIE'S OLD-FASHIONED SPICE CAKE

2 cups raisins
4 cups water (divided into 2)
5 cups flour
2 cups sugar
2 eggs
2 teaspoons baking soda
6 Tablespoons molasses
1 cup lard (Crisco all vegetable shortening; oil does not work)
1 teaspoon salt
1 teaspoon nutmeg
1 teaspoon cloves
1 teaspoon allspice
1 teaspoon cinnamon

Boil 2 cups raisins in 2 cups water for 20 minutes.

Thoroughly stir remaining ingredients and add to raisin and water mixture.
Pour into a well-greased tube or Bundt pan.
Bake 1 hour at 350 degrees.

EASY PINEAPPLE CAKE

Cake:
Follow directions on box of yellow or white cake mix and bake.

Frosting:
2 20-ounce cans crushed pineapple; drain juice (juice from canned pineapple for frosting may be substituted for water in cake recipe)
1 can condensed milk
2 Tablespoons squeezed fresh lemon juice

Combine pineapple and condensed milk, add lemon juice and stir.
Set for approximately 30 minutes until thick.
Frost cake.

Don't let your worries get the best of you. Remember, Moses started out as a basket case.

RED VELVET CAKE

1 teaspoon vinegar
1 Tablespoon baking powder
½ cup shortening (Crisco all-vegetable shortening; not oil)
1-½ cup sugar
2 eggs
1 teaspoon salt
3 teaspoons cocoa
1 teaspoon vanilla
2 ounces red food color
2-¼ cup flour
1 cup buttermilk (not low fat)

Preheat oven to 350 degrees.
Mix vinegar and baking powder. Set aside.

Beat together shortening, sugar, eggs, salt, cocoa, and vanilla until light and fluffy.
Beat in food color, add alternately flour and buttermilk.

Fold in vinegar and baking powder mixture.
Pour into greased and floured pans.
Bake 30 to 35 minutes.

CHALK WHITE FROSTING

1 cup fresh milk
¼ cup flour
1 cup regular (granulated) sugar
2 sticks margarine
2 teaspoons vanilla extract
1 teaspoon brandy extract

Stir milk and flour over medium heat until thick; let cool.

Separately beat with electric mixer: sugar and margarine, until fluffy.
Add cool cooked mixture.
Beat at high speed with mixer until smooth.
Fold in vanilla extract and brandy extract.

Keep refrigerated.

"FORBIDDEN FRUITS CREATE MANY JAMS"

Collins Gray Jr. is our family jelly connoisseur. His knowledge comes from a family of good cooks and much trial and error. He is always ready to share his sweet secrets with us, and we are always willing guinea pigs.

JELLY VARIATIONS

Ingredients listed below and process follows.

Blackberry Jelly

4 quarts berries to yield 4 cups juice
5 ½ cups sugar

Yields enough jelly for six 8-ounce jars

Pear Jelly

4 pounds pears, peeled
2-½ cups water to yield 4 cups juice
1 Tablespoon cinnamon (more or less if desired)
1 Tablespoon lemon juice
5-½ cups sugar
1 box fruit pectin

Yields enough jelly for eight 8-ounce jars

Wild Plum Jelly

These are the small reddish-yellow plums that are commonly seen growing in fields and in southern neighborhoods.

6 pounds plums to yield 5-½ cups juice
7-½ cups sugar
1 box fruit pectin

Yields enough jelly to fill eight 8-ounce jars

Grape Jelly

Muscadine (wild or cultivated purple grape, prevalent in eastern North Carolina) or scuppernong (wild or cultivated yellowish-green grape, prevalent on Hatteras Island). These are not to be confused with the common Concord grape.

3-½ to 4 pounds grapes to yield 5 cups of juice
7 cups sugar
1 box fruit pectin

Yields enough jelly for eight 8-ounce jars

GENERAL PROCEDURES FOR JELLIES

1. Rinse and then crush the designated quantity of fruit or berries in a large pot. Simmer for 10 minutes.
2. Place several layers of cheesecloth over a large measuring cup and secure with a large rubber band or clothespins.
3. Spoon the juice onto the cheesecloth and let it filter.
4. Repeat spooning until you have the number of cups of juice listed in the recipe. If necessary, up to ½ cup of water may be added to reach recommended volume.
5. Carefully remove and discard the cheesecloth, then pour the juice into a large pot and slowly mix in the fruit pectin.
6. While constantly stirring, bring to a full boil over high heat.

7. Quickly add the sugar, continue stirring, and return to a full boil for 1 minute.
8. Remove from the heat and, using a large spoon, skim the foam off the surface.
9. Fill sterilized jars to within ¼ inch of top. Clean the jar rim with wet cloth if any jelly spills.
10. Place new lid on jar, then firmly screw on the band.
11. Let the jars cool at room temperature. As they cool, you may hear a "pop" as the lids seal. If a jar does not properly seal, refrigerate instead of storing in the cupboard.

THANKS TO COLLINS GRAY JR.

FIG PRESERVES

This recipe may also be used for peaches and pears.

8 or 9 quarts blemish-free figs, washed and trimmed
4 pounds sugar
1 teaspoon salt
2 lemons, sliced thin

Cook all ingredients on medium heat until it turns into a thick syrup. Put in sterilized jars and seal.

Yields approximately 8 or 9 pints.

OLD-FASHIONED STRAWBERRY PRESERVES

Preparation time: 10 minutes
Cooking time: 25 minutes
Standing time: 6 hours

2 quarts small, ripe strawberries, washed, hulled
6 cups sugar
⅛ teaspoon salt
2 tablespoons light corn syrup
¼ cup fresh lemon juice

Yields approximately 5 cups

Put strawberries in a large (8-quart) non-aluminum saucepan with sugar, salt, and corn syrup.

Let stand at room temperature 5 to 6 hours.

Prepare home canning jars and lids according to manufacturer's directions.

Slowly heat strawberry mixture; cook and stir until sugar dissolves. After sugar dissolves, shake saucepan occasionally but do not stir.

Boil rapidly 15 to 25 minutes until, when pan is tilted, the liquid at the bottom has a tendency to set. Remove pan from heat. Skim foam. Cool. Stir in lemon juice.

Carefully ladle berries into hot prepared jars, leaving quarter-inch head space. Adjust caps according to manufacturer's directions. Process jars in a boiling water bath for 15 minutes. Remove; cool to room temperature on a cloth.

Check seal.
Store in cool dark place.

"Doubtless God could have made a better berry; but doubtless God never did," author Izaak Walton wrote 300 years ago.

He was speaking not only for himself but for many millions of strawberry lovers, including England's Queen Victoria, who mourned, in her dotage, that the strawberries didn't taste as good as they had when she was a girl.

Victoria should have tried our old-fashioned strawberry preserves on her royal taste buds. This strawberry jam is rich, thick, and heavy with the fresh, beautiful fruit of the season.

FIG MARMALADE

2 lemons, thinly sliced
2 pounds fresh figs, washed and blemish free, chopped
2 oranges, grated rind and juice
2 pounds sugar (4-½ cups)

In small saucepan, simmer lemon slices in water until tender. Drain.

Combine figs, juice and rind of oranges, and sugar in large pot. Bring to a boil and cook over low heat for 15 minutes, stirring occasionally.

Add drained lemons.

Continue to cook slowly until thick.
Seal in hot sterile jars.

FIG CAKE

2 cups sugar
1 cup chopped pecans
1 cup cooking oil
1 teaspoon salt
3 eggs
1 teaspoon baking soda
1 cup buttermilk
1 teaspoon cinnamon
2 cups all-purpose flour
1 teaspoon ginger
1 cup cooked figs or 1 pint fig preserves
1 teaspoon allspice

Combine all ingredients in order listed, and beat for 2 minutes at medium speed.
Pour into well-greased tube pan and bake 1 hour at 350 degrees.

If you have never tasted hot biscuits and homemade jelly or preserves you have missed one of the finer things in life.

SWEET POTATO BISCUITS

½ cup cooked and mashed sweet potatoes
½ cup sugar
½ cup butter, melted
2 Tablespoons milk
3-½ to 4 cups flour
1 teaspoon salt
4-½ teaspoons baking powder
1 Tablespoon cinnamon

Mix sweet potatoes, sugar, butter, and milk in a large bowl.
Combine flour, salt, baking powder, and cinnamon.
Blend in with sweet potato mixture.

Knead until the mixture doesn't stick to your fingers.
Roll out the dough on a floured counter to about ½-inch thick.
Cut out the biscuits with a biscuit or cookie cutter and place on a greased cookie sheet.

Bake in a 400-degree oven, on the middle rack, for 14 minutes.
Makes 18 biscuits.

At times my life seems bitter to the taste.
At times my cup of life seems empty.
We share who we are in conversation,
as we speak of life, it's gains and losses
and my cup is refilled.
The taste of bitterness turns sweet. You are good medicine.

VIOLA RUELKE GOMMER

RECIPE FOR A GOOD LIFE

Take a bit of thoughtfulness
Blend it with a smile.
Stir in a lot of kindness
as you tread life's weary mile.
Mix encouragement with some sunshine
to dry up someone's tears.
Stir in a few kind words of sympathy that
are certainly most sincere.
Then your reward will be great in heaven
and your life free from strife.
If you will follow this recipe for a good and useful life.

LEONA MEEKINS WILLIAMS

Love

Love is like the devil, because it torments us; like heaven, because it wraps the soul in bliss; like salt, because it is relishing; like pepper, because it often sets one on fire; like sugar, because it is sweet; like a rope, because it is often the death of man; like a prison, because it makes one miserable; like wine, because it makes us happy; like a man, because it is here today and gone tomorrow; like a woman, because there is no getting rid of it; like a beacon, because it guides one to the wished-for port; like a will-o'-the-wisp, because it often leads one into a bog; like a fierce courser, because it often runs away with one; like a little pony, because it ambles nicely with one; like the bite of a mad dog, or like the kiss of a pretty woman, because

> they both make a man mad; like a goose, because it is silly; like a rabbit, because there is nothing like it. In a word, it is like a ghost, because it is like everything and like nothing—often talked about, but never seen, touched, or understood.
>
> MORROW'S ALMANACK, 1929

We hope these recipes will stir fond memories of a bygone era with you and stimulate your interest in southern cooking. Some of these recipes are a companion volume to Jackie Gray and Lois Miller, *Kinnakeet Cuisine* (2003).

DISCLAIMER

Our immense study on the genealogy of Kinnakeet has involved thorough research of Dare, Hyde, and Currituck County records, census reports, family Bibles, marriage records, obituaries, libraries, church records, old newspaper articles, military records, and every conceivable source available to verify this information. Information from a very informative book by Lois Meekins and Amy Gamiel, *Sacred to Their Memory* (a book on the cemeteries), has provided a wealth of information. Also, individuals who have contributed to our stories are noted throughout the book. Although our research is far from definitive, our goal is to preserve the rich history of our ancestors and to pass this information on to future generations. A special thanks to Danny Couch, our Hatteras Island historian, for assisting with the introduction on pages 15 and 16.

This research has been done in good faith. It is designed solely for the purpose of furthering our family history and should be treated as a guide. While the information contained herein is correct to the best of our knowledge, we apologize for any inaccuracies in this information. Thanks to all of those who have been a part of this endeavor. For those of you in your family tree, we wish you happy tree climbing.

Here at the conclusion of our book we look back to "In the Beginning." Scripture tells us God is Alpha, the beginning, and Omega, the end. So what does eternity hold for us in view of what storms are brewing in our world today?

Revelation 22:13: "I am the Alpha and the Omega, the First and the Last, the Beginning and the End."

The first and last letters of the Greek alphabet, alpha and omega, offer a symbolic way of referring to God and his position as Lord over all history, from beginning to end.

Revelation 21:6: "And he also said, 'It is finished! I am the Alpha and the Omega—the Beginning and the End. To all who are thirsty I will give freely from the springs of the water of life.'"

What is that living water? If you have not tasted that fresh living water, may we encourage you to do so today. Thirsty souls who want God in their lives and their sins forgiven through Jesus Christ can "take the water of life without cost" (Revelation 22:17). "Whoever calls on the name of the Lord shall be saved" (Romans 10:13). Call upon Him and quench your thirst. Salvation is a free gift of God, received by faith. The choice you make about Jesus is the most important decision you will ever make on this Earth.

If you haven't asked Jesus to forgive your sin and give you eternal life, I invite you to pray, "Dear God, thank you for sending Your Son Jesus to die on the cross for my sins. I confess I am a sinner, and I ask You for Your forgiveness. Today I want to trust Jesus as my Lord and Savior. I give my life and future to You. In Jesus' name I pray, Amen."

May God Bless,
Lois Gray Miller and Barbara Meekins Austin

POSTSCRIPT

Oh, and those flowers on the cover . . .

Three days before my illness of August 2004 that sent me to the hospital, God had spoken to me in a mighty way. I experienced something so life-changing that it was seared in my heart, brain, and my very being, although I never disclosed this to anyone.

As I was walking through my bedroom, I heard the voice of God (in my spirit) that was so overwhelming it was difficult for me to stand upright.

It seemed like an eternity, but I am sure it was only minutes during which I experienced this manifestation of the Spirit.

One day I would write a book and share my story—not just my story, but the story of others as well.

In my mind I was even given a picture of the cover of the book. *Flowers!* At the time I did not realize the significance of the flowers or that there was even a language of flowers. As part of that circle, the first reading of the season for the Yellow House Ministry book club event of 2012 was chosen by Dr. Andrea Facci. You guessed it: *The Language of Flowers.* I went on a quest to find out the significance of these flowers. A horticulturist I am not. I love flowers, but taking care of them is not in my genes.

Although the flowers were of a common variety I did not know their names. I had to research pictures to find out what I was going to paint. Now I understand there is also a meaning to the exquisite beauty that God created.

Gerbera Daisy (pink flowers). The daisy symbolizes the innocence of the Christ Child and also purity and cheerfulness.

Joe Bells–Indian Blanket–Gaillardia pulchella. Joe Bell is a red flower with yellow tips that grows wild and is an uncultivated flowering plant.

"Uncle Joe Bell" is credited with populating the island with gaillardias or "Joe Bell Flowers." Joe Bell lived in Washington, North Carolina. His lover was not considered good enough for him, so his parents sent him away. Upon his return to Washington, he found she had married another. He came to Ocracoke to mourn his loss, and while there he sowed the seed of this beautiful flower all over the island. He died on the island, and to this day the flower carries his name throughout the Outer Banks. No one really knows for sure if the story is true, but we do know that a man by the name of Joe Bell did exist and is buried on Ocracoke Island.

So what we have is an uncultivated wild child cheerfully embraced by individuals through the love of Jesus Christ with purity and cheerfulness. That love gives us hope for the future.

CPSIA information can be obtained
at www.ICGtesting.com
Printed in the USA
LVHW081151241122
733912LV00015B/666

9 781597 152532